# Township School Trustees and Treasurers in Illinois

## 1819-1980

Charles W. Clabaugh
With the Assistance of
Randy DeVillez
and
John Wm. Martin

# Table of Contents

# Remarks

Illinois has had a rich educational history. It is the story of a commitment to quality education evolved from complex interactions between institutions, personalities, and societal forces. An important theme in this development has been the struggle for organizational efficiency in the governance of education, as the roles of officials have been refined to meet new demands. This trend is clearly illustrated by the historical development of the township school trustees and treasurers, the two oldest school officers in the State. Today these executives serve only in Cook County, because the offices are not deemed efficient for counties with a population under one million. This situation is quite different from that which existed in the early years of Illinois, when these positions were an integral part of the township organization of the Northwest Ordinance.

Former State Representative Charles W. Clabaugh has provided a comprehensive summary of the change in Illinois history with this volume. His contribution is a useful and functional compendium of turning points in the legal development of the two offices. The book details their changing roles and duties, as well as their relationship to other educational officials including directors of school boards. The study is a chronological digest, but it also contains interesting sidelights on Illinois education. For example, the role of women in the early governance of education is noted. Other important themes such as the development of school funds form a background for the narrative.

Illinois Superintendents of Education have always worked closely with the township trustees and treasurers. In the late nineteenth century, for example, the early Superintendents of Public Instruction depended on these front-line executives for detailed information and statistics about the operations of a fledgling educational system. The correspondence of the State Superintendents housed in the State Archives Building details the mutual concerns they shared. For example, James Park Slade, superintendent from 1878-1882, worked cooperatively with township treasurers in seeking census information from localities. In one letter he urged treasurers to use "*suasive* force" to gather statistical data.

The trustees and treasurers have been engaged in educational governance in a number of ways. Not the least of these is the provision of an outside look at the fiscal affairs of school districts. We should be indebted to Mr. Clabaugh for assembling these highlights of Illinois' search for educational efficiency and excellence. His book is testimony to the reality that the roles of educational officials can evolve to serve better the citizens of Illinois.

---

*Remarks by Joseph M. Cronin, Illinois State Superintendent of Education*

STATE OF ILLINOIS

# OFFICE OF THE GOVERNOR

SPRINGFIELD 62706

JAMES R. THOMPSON
GOVERNOR

March 1979

Friends of Education:

As we in Illinois address the education issues which are likely to have impact in the decade of the 1980's, we are fortunate to be able to draw upon a sound educational history and tradition.

Our educational past can rightly be characterized as having been hewed out of sound driving principles: a strong community voice in local school policies, a local and state partnership in funding the common schools, and outstanding leadership in the General Assembly for enhancing high quality educational programs throughout Illinois. Charles W. Clabaugh's book captures a key portion of our past, the historical development of School Trustees and Treasurers. I am pleased to commend this book to your careful reading and reflection.

Sincerely,

James R. Thompson
GOVERNOR

JRT:klk

**State of Illinois**

**Illinois Office of Education**
Springfield, Illinois 62777

**Joseph M. Cronin**
State Superintendent of Education

April 26, 1979

Mr. Lawrence E. Hupe
President
Cook County School
  Treasurers Association
12720 South Western Avenue
Blue Island, Illinois 60406

Dear Mr. Hupe:

The Clabaugh manuscript has been reviewed by Dr. William Gillies and
myself. We attach the enclosed remarks which confirm the usefulness of
the work for future historians and researchers. You may use these
comments in the bound volume. Thank you for the privilege of reviewing
this book in advance of publication. We would appreciate a hard bound
copy for our state education library.

Sincerely,

Joseph M. Cronin
State Superintendent
of Education

Enclosures

# EDUCATIONAL SERVICE REGION
# COOK COUNTY

33 West Grand Avenue
Chicago, Illinois 60610

(312) 443-5000

**RICHARD J. MARTWICK**
Superintendent of Schools

March 14, 1979

Mr. Lawrence E. Hupe
President
Cook County School Treasurers Association
12720 South Western Avenue
Blue Island, Illinois 60406

Dear Mr. Hupe:

    If it were not for the work of a dedicated and energetic
few, there would be far too few perspectives of history.
Therefore, my compliments to former Representative Clabaugh
and the Township School Trustees and Treasurers Association
of Cook County for providing future generations with an
evolutionary look at both offices and the people and issues
surrounding them.

Best Wishes,

Richard J. Martwick
Superintendent

RJM/kbz

8

To the Trustees and Treasurers
who have served the needs of
Education in the State of Illinois
throughout the years.

## Acknowledgments

The Trustees and Treasurers would like to acknowledge the Illinois State Assemblies' foresight in adapting the original laws to conform to todays needs and tommorrows challenges.

# Preface

This study presents the history of the two oldest school offices in the State of Illinois—School Trustee and Treasurer—by detailing the legal basis which established them and which changed their composition and function through the more than century and a half of their existence. Upon this legal skeleton, these township officers and their constituents put the flesh and blood which grew into the System of Public Education in Illinois.

In addition, this study contains a discussion of some of the collateral enactments which played a direct part in defining the roles of the Trustees and Treasurers. For example, there is a lengthy treatment of the origin of the two principal early school funds.

To undertake a study of this type—both as writer and as reader—it is necessary to keep in mind the beginnings and the legal foundation of American education. Many people feel that the framers of the Federal Constitution purposely omitted any reference to public education because they viewed it as a function of the state and not of the Federal Government. As this study suggests, it would seem more probably that not many people, including the Constitution's writers, considered education as a function or responsibility of any government unit, but rather as the responsibility of the parents or the church, as it had been traditionally.

This view encourages more respect for those early Township Trustees and Treasurers who were the fledgling administrators of an untried and untested system, a system created by a fledgling legislature, an educational system without precedent. The responsibilities of these early officers were enormous.

For the first six years, their responsibilities related to school land administration. Collectively, the officers had almost a million acres of land scattered over tens of thousands of square miles. The land was first to be rented, and then to be rented or sold, all for the purpose of fostering education. It wasn't until the passage of the Free School Act of 1825 that the officers were given any school duties. This act was interpreted as entrusting them with the general superintendency of the schools of their township, though some authorities disagree.

There were two short periods, in 1833 and 1841, when there were two sets of Trustees in the same townships: one "Trustees of School Lands," and the other "Trustees of Schools."

From these complex and confused beginnings emerged school districts with their Boards of Directors. Trustees were gradually relieved of the administrative functions of their districts and their schools; they came to act as go-betweens in the districts and the county, while retaining their duties as administrators of the school lands. In addition, for a brief time, the Treasurer legally was entrusted with general supervision of the schools of his township. This fact points to a difficulty in researching a study of this type: at times the statutes used the terms "Trustee" and "Director" interchangeably, making it somewhat difficult to determine to whom the legislature intended to give certain rights and duties. The same difficulty arises with the terms "organized counties" and "incorporated townships." It is important to remember that some counties in Illinois originally extended almost from the Ohio River to the present Wisconsin state line and beyond.

As this preface has indicated and the text reveals, the passing of decades and the enactment of laws have aided the emergence and development of a great school system. Only the school Trustees and Treasurers have been with it since its inception.

The office of School Trustee is the oldest school office in the State of Illinois. The office was created by the first session of the First General Assembly of this state, by an act approved March 2, 1819.[1] There were to be three Trustees, each appointed by the County Commissioner for a term of four years. The Trustees were to appoint a Treasurer; thus this office is the second oldest school office in Illinois. The law did not set a specific term of office for the Treasurer, who was to serve at the pleasure of the Trustees.[2] Illinois is the only state to ever have Township School Treasurers. The terms of office of both of these officers were to remain as fixed by this act until 1833, and the number of Trustees until 1837.

These offices were so interwoven in the fabric of education and its laws—both federal and state—in early Illinois that it is important to outline the genesis of both. A background is found in digests of some of the most significant of these acts, such as *Building the State Common School Fund in Illinois* by the Illinois Education Association.:

UNITED STATES CONGRESS—ACT OF APRIL 18, 1818: To enable Illinois to form a Constitution and state government; offered sixteenth section of each township for school use of inhabitants thereof; granted certain saline lands to state; granted 5% of net proceeds of public lands sold after January 1, 1819, of which two-fifths of proceeds were to be used for federal roads and three-fifths (less one-sixth of the same for a college or university) were to be used for the encouragement of learning: 36 sections granted for a seminary of learning (as well as the township heretofore reserved.)

ILLINOIS—CONVENTION OF AUGUST 26, 1818: Accepted the above offered propositions of the federal government regarding land grants.[3]

It is apparent, then, that two sources of income for the schools were provided for in the above act: (1) The funds obtained from the sale or use of the sixteenth section solely for the use of schools in the township where this land lay. (2) The permanent Common School Fund of the state, the interest from which was to be divided among the counties, according to law, for the benefit of the schools, therein. Some of the very early state acts dealt with the sixteenth section grant.

The State Act of 1819, referred to in the first paragraph, titled "An Act Relating to the Land Reserved for the Use of Schools," directed the County Commission in each and every county to appoint three Trustees in each (congressional) township, whose population would admit such appointment, for a period of four years.[4] The "sixteenth section" referred to was "that section numbered sixteen, in every township (in the state) granted to the state, (by the federal government) for the use of the inhabitants of the township, for the use of the schools."[5] The "Township Loanable Fund" was the name given to the fund derived from sale, rent, or any other source of income from the sixteenth section.

The Act of 1819 further directed the Trustees to employ a competent surveyor to lay out the land in section sixteen of each township in lots of not less than forty acres nor more than 160, which land would be leased for a period of not more than ten years, or rented, the income obtained to be used for school purposes.[6] Timber growing on such land was to be preserved and protected upon a penalty of $8.00 or $3.00 per tree or sapling, depending on the kind which was cut, felled, boxed, bored, or destroyed by trespassers.[7] This act was general law, applicable in each and every county in Illinois.

It is important to remember that prior to 1870, much legislation in the state was of a private or special nature, applicable to a single county, township, city or (in some instances) a person. The provisions of these acts depended, to a great extent, upon the request made of the legislature, by the petitioners; furthermore, the act passed which granted the petition applied only to the petitioning body, and their provisions did not necessarily correspond to those enacted for other bodies of a similar nature, or to general law.

Reprinted below is the preamble to, and a digest of, some provisions of one of these special acts, passed and approved January 30, 1821, in answer to a petition of the inhabitants of the town of Alton. This specific act empowered town trustees different in number from those required by general law with duties relating to school land, though not section sixteen powers, and with duties relating to church land.

Very significantly, these trustees were authorized to levy a tax for various school functions, which in all probability made it the first such authorization in the history of Illinois. Again, this was a private act, applicable only to the town of Alton.

> Whereas, the inhabitants of the town of Alton, in the County of Madison, have presented their petition to this legislature, setting forth, that the original proprietors of said town did make a donation of one hundred town lots, one-half for the support of the gospel, and the other half for the support of public schools in said town forever, which said town lots rest at present in the patentees of the tract on which said town is situated, and who are not authorized to use the said donation for the purposes intended by the donor; and whereas the said petitioners have prayed that the said town may be incorporated and trustees appointed in whom and their successors the said lots may rest forever, to be used and applied agreeably to the purposes intended; and the objects of said petitioners appearing just and reasonable; therefore, be it enacted, . . .[8]

These trustees were also authorized to appoint a treasurer.[9]

Another act from this time period, "An Act to Encourage Learning in White County, And for Other Purposes" also dealt with school lands. This act approved February 14, 1821, is reprinted below in its entirety.

> Whereas there is a society of Christians called 'Cumberland Presbyterians', who have erected a meeting-house for public worship on the sixteenth section in township five south of range eight east of the third principle meridian in this state, and whereas the said house may serve to have the gospel preached therein, and likewise may be used as a schoolhouse for the township: Therefore,*Sec. I.* Be it resolved by the people of the State of Illinois, represented in the General Assembly, that two or more of the County Commissioners of White County are hereby authorized and required to lease five acres of land of the said section sixteen in township five south, range eight east, including said meeting-house and burial ground, to the trustees of the township for ninety-nine years, for use of said society of Cumberland Presbyterians, and for use of school of said township. *Sec. II.* Be it further enacted, that the said school which may be taught in the said _____ shall be under the direction of the trustees of the township and said society of Cumberland Presbyterians. There shall never be given any preference to one sect of people over another in said school, but at all times the said society of Cumberland Presbyterians shall be entitled to hold divine service in said house during said lease.[10]

An examination of the school laws prior to the Free School Act of 1825 will show that the powers and duties of Trustees created by the Act of 1819 were to govern the school land and to appointment of a Recording Clerk, a Treasurer, and a Surveyor of the School Land. The special acts of 1821, however, created the Trustees in the town of Alton, and the White County Act, cited above, gave general powers of school superintendence to the Trustees, but in only the two locations named.

The school Trustee and Treasurers were destined to play a much larger role in the development of Illinois schools. Their increased role came about as a result of the second source of income provided for the schools when Illinois was young: the Permanent School Fund.In Illinois, this fund historically has been made up of two chief components: (1) The 3% fund granted by the United States from the sale of public lands within the state, and, (2) The surplus revenue fund of 1836.

The Illinois Education Association's 1943 publication, *Building the Common School Fund,*[11] is a digest of federal and state enactments which influenced and affected the schools of Illinois. Included are the following important acts:

UNITED STATES CONGRESS—ACT OF DECEMBER 12, 1820: Provided that the U.S. Secretary of the Treasury pay 3% of the net proceeds of public lands sold in Illinois to persons authorized by the Legislature of Illinois to receive the same for the encouragement of learning, such payments be made quarterly when money was available. It contained the requirement that the annual account of the use of the same should be made to the U.S. Secretary of the Treasury or else payments would be withheld.

ILLINOIS—ACT OF 1821: Authorized the State Treasurer to receive the 3% fund for the encouragement of learning, and transfer the same to state bank, said bank to pay 6% interest. Federal authority gave an order for the first payment on the 3% fund on December 27, 1821.

ILLINOIS—JANUARY 1, 1823 REPORT OF STATE TREASURER: Shows the record of a draft on the bank of Illinois for $2,955.82 and draft of $3,000 on receiver of public monies at Kaskaskia, said drafts being from the U.S. Treasurer on account of the 3% fund. It also shows the record and tells the story of Treasurer M'Laughlin and Dr. Duncan's trip and their expenses in cashing the two drafts, the net sum of which was $5,804.87—one-half being received into the State Treasury as the beginning of the permanent common school fund of Illinois. The first draft, cashed at the State Bank of Illinois March 1, 1882, netted $2,846.87. The second draft cashed August 20, 1822, netted $2,958.00. The story of the first money coming into the common school fund and of the first expense upon the fund for such items as "horse feed" and "pine boxes" is told on pages 229 and 230 of *Laws of Illinois,* 1823 in the section containing the report submitted by the State Treasurer. The exact quotation from such pages is as follows:

1822
Feb. To    14 days of wagon and horses to convey

money from Shawneetown to Vandalia, including horse feed, at $4.00 per day, Cash    56.00
"    paid Dr. Duncan, for going to Shawneetown,    25.00
"    Expense of self and Dr. Duncan 14 days at $1.75 per day    25.00
"    Cash paid Secretary of State for transcript of Bank law of the State Bank of Illinois,    11.57

Note principle of early federal legislation such as Ordinance of 1785, etc.

Aug. "    Going to Kaskaskia for residue of money in the hands of the Receiver at that place, with wagon and horses, 8 days at $4.00 per day,    32.00
"    3 pine boxes to put the money in, at 4s 6d    2.25

$151.82

CR. By cash retained out of the three percent fund for the use of schools,    150.94-½
By amount of the two certificates of the Cashier of the State Bank of Illinois, brought down,    5804.87-½
Amount received from the United States R. K. M'Laughlin, Treasurer.    $5955.82

ILLINOIS—ACT OF 1825: Permanent common school fund (called the 3% fund) nominally passed to the Commissioners of the School Fund (Auditor, Secretary of State, and Governor) by the 1825 Act but really remained on deposit in State Bank. Also the 1825 Act stated that the interest covering five-sixths of the 3% fund should go to the counties of Illinois in proportion to the number of white inhabitants under 21 years of age and that it should be spent for schools.

ILLINOIS—ACT OF 1829: Provided that Governor should borrow the principal of the 3% fund at 6% interest, the interest to be added to the principal each year until refunded. Thus, the interest was diverted from the schools by this Act.

Following this enactment, it would appear that from 1829 until 1835 no interest from the permanent fund was paid to the schools, as evidenced by the following passages:

"ROW" SETTLED IN 1831: U.S. Secretary of the Treasury withheld the 3% fund due Illinois as no annual account of deposition of same was being made to said Secretary. Governor Edwards admitted that Illinois was diverting the 3% fund for the state's current expenses. A long "row" developed. The U.S. Congress by Act of January 13, 1831 repealed that part of the Federal Act of December 12, 1820 which required such annual accounting.

ILLINOIS—ACT OF FEBRUARY 7, 1835: Legislature ordered accrued interest on 3% fund to be added to the principal and that interest on said fund at 6% a year should go to the counties for school use in proportion
to the number of white persons under 21 years of age.

PAYMENT WITHHELD IN 1846: Payments on 3% fund temporarily withheld in 1846 in case of states which
were default on their state bonds held by United States
in trust.

LAST PAYMENT IN 1863: The last record of payment on the 3% fund was September 28, 1863. Total payments on the 3% fund were $712,745.34. Five-sixths of the fund (one-sixth being turned aside for college or university) amounted to $593,954.45 and interest added to principal amounted to $19,408.51; and hence that part of the 3% fund which helps to make up the state permanent common school fund is $613,362.96. Such is the record that still remains on the Auditor's books 77 years after the last payment of September 28, 1863.

**Surplus Revenue Fund**
UNITED STATES SURPLUS REVENUE FUND. The distribution of the surplus revenue fund in the federal treasury in 1837 is a matter of general history. By the Act of July 4, 1836, the U.S. Congress directed the Secretary of the Treasury in four quarterly installments to deposit with the several states—in proportion to their respective representation in Congress—all money in the U.S. Treasury in excess of $5,000,000 on January 1, 1837. The states were pledged to keep the same and repay it whenever it might be required by said Secretary. Three installments were paid but the fourth was never made. Illinois received $477,919.24.

The Tenth General Assembly of Illinois anticipating such payments ordered the State Treasurer to receive the same and place to the credit of the Fund Commissioners any balance of the surplus revenue that might remain after the state paid what it owed to the school, college, and seminary funds. The state owed the school funds $355,592.32 and such was all paid into the common school fund under direction of the State Auditor. Such payment was held to be an addition to the fund and not a payment of the debts due the several school funds by the state. Thus, the common school fund of that date was nearly doubled by the surplus revenue distribution.

**Permanent State Common School Fund: Two Parts**
Hence, the permanent state common school fund for many years has consisted of (1) five-sixths of 3% of the net proceeds of sale of public lands, amounting to $613,362.96 and (2) the surplus revenue distribution assigned to the school fund of $335,592.32. The total is $948,995.28. In reality, such exists as a state debt owed to the schools. A little over 6% on such amount is now being appropriated and paid from the general revenue fund yearly as interest on the permanent state school fund, the principal proper having been "borrowed" and used by the state to avoid statewide property taxes in early years. The sum of $57,000 is appropriated each year as 6% on the permanent school fund.

# 1825

The literature of the schools in Illinois indicates that there were disputed claims between various localities as to which had the first school in this state.[12] As stated, there were the special-act schools in Alton and in White County. There probably were others, but most that existed at that time were the result of well-to-do families employing teachers to instruct their children, usually in the home of one of the families in the community.

The issue of slavery also had its effects on the schools and school legislation. The fight against slavery in Illinois, was at that time, a sustained educational program carried on by such men as Governor Coles, General Duncan, and Reverend Peck. "These leaders believed that slavery and ignorance were the twin relics of barbarism. The surest way to save the state from the blight of slavery was through enlightenment . . . youth must be taught the evils of slavery and ignorance in free schools, provided by the state . . ."[13] This struggle lasted from 1818 to 1825, and ended in a victory for the anti-slavery cause. In this atmosphere, and partially because of it, the Free School Act of 1825 was enacted by the legislature. It was unique in that only a few eastern states had a free school law.[14]

The Free School Act of 1825 provided that there should be established a school or schools in each county of the state, which should be open and free to every class of white citizens between the ages of five and twenty-one; it also provided that persons over the age of twenty-one years, might be admitted on such terms as the Trustees of the district might prescribe,[15] and that school should be kept open at least three months out of each twelve.

Section II of the act provided that the County Commissioners' Court should from time to time form school districts . . . whenever a petition of a majority of voters requested it, but each such district should contain not less than fifteen families.[16]

The act further provided that the voters of the district thus established should elect three Trustees, one Clerk, one Treasurer, and one Assessor to serve at the pleasure of the Trustees.[17] By Section IV ". . . it [became] the duty of the Trustees to superintend the schools within their respective districts; to examine and employ teachers; to lease all land belonging to the district; to call meetings of the voters when they thought it expedient, or when asked to do so by five legal voters; to report to the County Commissioners' Court . . . the number of children living within the bounds of said district between the ages of five and twenty-one years, and what number of them [were] actually sent to school, with a certificate of the time a school is actually kept . . . and the probably expense of the same."[18]

The other officers were given the duties signified by their title: the Clerk to keep a record of the meetings, the Assessor to assess the property of the district, the Collector to collect taxes, and after retaining five percent for his services, pay the balance to the Treasurer, who was empowered to pay out money upon written vouchers ordered by the Trustees, or by the citizens assembled in general meetings provided by this act.[20]

While the legislature, through this act, gave general superintendence of these schools to the Trustees, it is evident that the legislature also gave legal authority to the general meeting of the legal voters of the district to authorize the Treasurer to pay out money upon order of the meeting.

Also in Section XII, the act gave to the general meeting in incorporated townships, the specific authority to levy a tax of either cash or produce, not to exceed one-half per centum, nor amounting to more than $10 on any person, for establishment and support of the schools within their district.

The method of deciding upon the rate of the tax as to permit each voter present to propose a rate, the highest to be voted on first, and in case of disagreement, upon the next highest, and so on, until a majority of all legal voters within the district, so-taxed, did agree.[21]

It can be assumed that the development of the offices of Boards of School Directors and School Boards was a result of the general meeting feature of this Act of 1825.

Most significant in this landmark Act of 1825 was Section XV, which provided for a specific portion of state funds to be added to the local property tax cited above for school purposes. Section XV stated:

> That for the encouragement and support of schools, respectively established within this state, according to this act, there shall be appropriated, for that purpose, two dollars out of every hundred hereafter to be received in the treasury of this state; also, five-sixths of the interest arising from the school fund, which is to be distributed to the different counties of the state in proportion to the number of white inhabitants in each county under twenty-one years of age.[22].

The Trustees were to collect the rents obtained from school lands and divide this amount among the inhabitants of the townships in proportion to the sum that each had contributed in tax, subscriptions, or otherwise to the support of the school.[23]

The State Auditor and the Secretary of State, under the Governor, were constituted Commissioners of the School Fund, and were entitled to receive all money paid to the state from the Treasury of the United States.

A total of 985,066 acres of sixteenth section land was granted to the States by the Federal Government for the benefit of the schools. In the statistical report of the Superintendent of Public Instruction, 1882, page CXXVII, W.E. Pillsburg stated that there were 8,513 acres in the state still unsold. The total estimated value of the unsold land, the receipts from land sold, and the accrued interest amounted to $8,018,936.31. The average price per acres of the land then sold was $3.78.[24]

In his book, *Development of the Free Public High School in Illinois,* referred to earlier in this study, Paul Belting states that there is very little evidence to show whether any free school districts were established under this act. He states that there are no published records of any money being appropriated out of state funds for the support of free schools.[25] He does document, however, that five free schools were established in Madison County in 1825.[26]

The Act of 1825 did affect the Trustees and Treasurer: three Trustees were to be elected by the people and they were empowered with the general superintendence of the schools in their districts; since no term of office was mentioned, it is assumed that the four year term was to be continued. There was no appreciable change in the powers of the Treasurer, but, by terms of this act, that officer was to be elected by the voters during the general meeting.

# 1826

A short act of three sections, of some interest to the curious, was passed and approved in January of 1826. It provided that "the (state) Treasurer shall pay . . . to the Commissioners of the School Fund . . . the sum of one thousand and thirty seven dollars and seventy-nine cents . . . as full restitution of that portion of the school fund which has been robbed from the state bank, and not recovered . . ."[27]

# 1827

Apparently, the provisions of the Free School Act were too advanced for the legislature, and accordingly, in 1827, that body repealed the local tax portion of the act and, instead, provided for taxation, only with the consent of those to be taxed. It did provide, however, that no one could send a "scholar" to the school unless he paid a tax.[28] The legal voters, at their regular meeting, were given the power through use of discretion, to cause either the whole or one-half of the sum required to support the school in the district, to be raised by taxation. If only one-half was to be raised by taxation, the remainder was required to be paid by parents, masters, and guardians.[29]

This repeal act, especially the section declaring that no person should be taxed without and until his consent had been had in writing, greatly weakened the Act of 1825 and had the potential of destroying the cause of free schools. Whether the superintendence of the schools by the Trustees and whether the general meeting of the voters were left in the law or repealed is a matter of interpretation.

The Treasurer was to receive any donation of money or personal property and the "avails always [were] to be used [in the] district."[30] This enactment permitted tuition contribution by parents of attending pupils.

In 1827, the legislature's interest in the schools seemed to be centered more on the school lands than on the schools. A second act approved less than three months after the first, provided that three Trustees be appointed by the County Commissioners' Court in each township where deemed expedient. The Trustees were to be called "Trustees of School Lands."[31] The protection and the preservation of school lands and the timber, stone, and coal on or under it, were the primary duties of the Trustees, as set forth by the Acts of 1827.

The Trustees were further directed to appoint and to discharge, at their pleasure, a Clerk and, when expedient, a Treasurer.[32] They should, as soon as they deemed it expedient, lay off school districts, none of which were to have [fewer] than eighteen "scholars" attending school, provided that no township was to be laid off into a school district, unless by a petition of a majority of the free holders of the township.[33]

18

# 1829

The school laws of 1829 completed the legislature's economic action begun during the former session. The new laws took from the schools the remaining financial support given them by federal and state laws. As pointed out, the 1827 session amended the local tax feature of the 1825 Act by permitting this tax only by consent of those to be taxed. In 1829, the entire local tax section was repealed.[34] Also repealed at that session was the provision that required rents from school land to be used only for school purposes.[35] This land was to be sold by a Commissioner appointed by the County Commissioners' Court. Thus, the Trustees lost control of the school land.[36] The land was to be sold on petition signed by nine-tenths of the citizens of the township, and none was to be sold for less than one dollar and twenty-five cents per acre.[37]

The Commissioner was instructed to take the money received from the sale of this land and loan it on interest at the highest obtainable rate. Furthermore, the Commissioner was to pay to the Trustees the money received from the original sale. The law is ambiguous as to how the Trustees were to use these funds, but the law was quite clear that only the interest and not the principal should be used for township purposes.[38]

This act's devastating effects on the economics of school land was compounded by the greed of

land grabbers and the pressures applied by persons living on these lands. The final section (XI) of this act provided that any land not sold at public sale "[could] be purchased [from the] Commissioner at private sale." The legislators apparently sensed the danger of fraud inherent in this section and set forth provisions for the prosecution of wrongdoers.[39]

This act, although very harmful to the schools' economy, was passed five days after another act which proved to be even more destructive—if not disgraceful—toward the schools. This prior act provided that the Commissioners of the school fund (Governor, Auditor, and Secretary of State) would loan to the state all the money in the school fund. Furthermore, the six percent interest to be paid by the state would be added to the principal and the entire amount would be borrowed by the state until it was refunded.[40]

Thus, the schools lost even the interest on that portion of the permanent school fund derived from three percent of the returns from public lands. The money was used by the state for current expenditures. Many of the researchers and scholars of this phase of the state's history conclude that this was done in an effort to avoid a direct tax for general state purposes. "From this time (1829) to the passage of the Free School Act of 1855, common schools were supported largely by the tuition paid by the parents."[41]

# 1831

In 1831, the County Commissioners' Court was directed to appoint three Trustees and a Treasurer and to restore most of the authority of the Trustees over school land, except that the Commissioner was empowered to sell it, upon petition of three-fourths of the white male inhabitants in the township.[42] Also, the Commissioner was to set the rate of interest to be charged

when money received from these sales was loaned.[43]

After all or portions of the school land had been sold, five or more citizens of the township could borrow $200 of the money, to be obtained from the Commissioner for the purpose of erecting a school.[44] This loan was to be repaid at an interest rate of six percent, probably with the tuition funds which the parents paid.

A half-hearted effort to restore some authority to the Trustees for superintendence of the schools seems to have been made in Section III of this act which stated: ". . . the trustees . . . [are] to do and perform so much of the duties of trustees set forth by that act (of 1827) as will be conducive to the advancement of common schools, in their township."[45]

Also included in the Act of 1831 was this interesting and far reaching provision:

Sec. 1: All gifts and grants made heretofore of land for the erection of a school-house, a house for divine worship, and for burying the dead, . . . not more than ten acres for church or burying-ground, shall be held in law to the use of the person or persons . . . for the purpose of education, for divine worship, or for the internmentof the dead, and no other.

Sec. 2: When grant of land is made for the above purposes, it shall be made and executed to the county commissioner . . . in trust and for the use of the persons or societies and for the purpose above mentioned.

Sec. 4: When such gift or grant is no longer used for the specified purpose, it shall vest in the county to be sold and proceeds applied to education in the county.[46]

## 1833

## 1833-1849
## Who Is Responsible-Who Will Fund?

The school act approved March 1, 1833, created Trustees whose sole function was the general superintendence of the school of the district. This is similar to a present-day school board.

The three Trustees were to be chosen by the employers of the teachers. They were to serve as Trustees of the schools of the district and their term of office was to be one year. They were to receive and apply to the use of the school any donation of money, books, maps, globes, stationery, or other articles necessary or useful for the schools. The Trustees were also instructed to ". . . require the admission into the school, and the gratuitous tuition of [any] children . . . [for whom the] . . . Trustees believed the parents . . . unable to pay tuition . . ."[47]

If any money was in the hands of the County School Commissioner, after he had paid for the survey and the sale of school land of the township, that money was to be apportioned to the teachers entitled to it.[48] Township funds were to be loaned by the Commissioner who would set the rate of interest, one-half year paid in advance.

The inclusion of this section in the Act of 1833 indicates the sad state of management, if not open fraud, prevalent in the handling and sale of school lands.

An earlier section of this book dealt with the Permanent School Fund. At that time it was stated that there were two main components, the first of which was discussed: the three percent fund granted by the United States from the sale of public lands within the state.

The other component was the Surplus Revenue Fund of 1836. This fund was brought to Illinois by an act of Congress, requiring the distribution of all money in excess of $5 million which had accumulated in the U.S. Treasury. The money was distributed to and deposited with the various states in proportion to population and it was to be repaid when requested. The request for repayment never came.

# 1835

The legislature of 1835 apparently anticipated the 1836 action of the U.S. Congress and provided by law, that the money would be received by the Commissioners of the School Fund, as a payment for money the state owed the schools; the Commissioners were to ". . . deposit the [money] in the state treasury to be used by the state for revenue purposes; and the state [would] be charged with the same, and with the interest . . ."[49]

Thus, once again, the legislature generously directed federal money to the school fund, but just as generously provided that it should be borrowed by the state for general revenue purposes. The legislature did, however, provide that six percent interest should be paid, by the state, to the Common School Fund.

As stated, the two parts of the Permanent School Fund totaled almost $949,000 by the time Illinois received the last payment from the United States in 1863. The interest amounted to $57,000 annually, which, historically, has been appropriated, year by year, to the Common School Fund. Of course, as the state appropriations to this fund rose into the millions of dollars, the inclusion of $57,000 really had only historic value, but it was a provision in every biennial appropriation to the Common School

Fund from 1873 until 1969[50] when it was omitted by the Bureau of the Budget which then began to draw these bills.

The rapidly accelerating population growth in Illinois from the middle 1830s onward is reflected in the ever-changing school laws passed by the legislature as it struggled to meet the demands for more schools in various parts of the state. The legislature extended considerable freedom to local communities to permit the establishment of schools but refused to permit the local authorities to levy a tax on everyone in the community to support the schools. At the same time, however, the legislature was unwilling to see that sufficient state money was channeled into the local schools in any appreciable amounts. In other words, the legislature appeared willing to try every possible means of financing schools, except the only two ways that would finance them: a general local tax and state financial assistance.

Historical records and accounts of this time in Illinois history are replete with charges of waste and fraud in the sale of school lands. In an effort to cope with this situation, the General Assembly made many changes in school land personnel and procedures.

# 1837

According to the Act of 1837, the Trustees of School Lands were to call an election in every township in the state. These elections allowed every legal voter to vote for or against the Township being incorporated for school purposes. A two-thirds favorable vote was necessary for incorporation. The approval was followed by an election to choose five freeholders of the township, known as "Trustees of the Schools." These Trustees were to superintend the township's business affairs for education

and schools and were to be successors of the former Trustees of School Lands in the township. Their term of office was to be two years and they were to have general superintendence of all schools in the township. These Trustees of Schools were to be a corporate body and were to have perpetual succession.[51]

In July and January, the Trustees were to meet to apportion equally among the teachers the interest accruing from the township funds. Any money left over was to be added to the township fund.[52] No teacher was to be paid out of the school fund unless he or she had obtained from the Trustees of his or her township a certificate of qualification to teach the [subject matter] taught by that teacher.[53]

The Trustees were authorized to appoint a Treasurer who would also serve as a Secretary. The term of office would be the same as that of the Trustees making the appointment. The Treasurer was to receive and pay out all money of the township and was to pay the teachers under the direction of the Trustees. The Treasurer was to give sufficient bond secured by two or more freeholders of the township.[54]

The Treasurer was considered the sole legal custodian of the township school funds.[55] This provision was repealed and reenacted several times by subsequent acts. With each reenactment, the provision remained basically unchanged.

The Act of 1837 provided that the interest accruing in the school fund should be distributed to the counties, presumably for the support of the schools.[56]

During the first week of July and January, the Treasurers of the township were to make abstracts of all schedules of the schools returned to them, showing the name of each teacher, the total number of scholars attending each school, and the total number of days taught. This information was submitted to the Trustees.[57]

The Act of 1837 defined the responsibilities of the County School Commissioner. (This position closely parallels that of the later-emerging County Superintendent of Schools.) The County School Commissioner was responsible for collecting detailed reports covering all aspects of the school operations, including financial condition, number and names of teachers, number of pupils, and number of days taught. Once collected, this information was sent to the State Auditor who presented it to the General Assembly which was responsible for holding all information pertaining to the condition of the schools in the state.[58]

# 1841

The Act of 1841 radically changed Illinois school laws. The act contained 108 sections and it repealed fifteen existing acts or parts of acts. For the first time, the management of school lands and the supervision of the interest obtained therefrom, were separated, for the most part, from the direction and general superintendence of the schools.

By Division 1 of this act the County Commissioners were given control and general supervision of all school lands in the county, including section sixteen and any other land owned by the township for school purposes. The County Commissioners were directed to appoint three Trustees in each township to be called "Trustees of School Lands." They were to be legal voters and inhabitants of the township, and [their] appointment was to be for four years. These Trustees of School Lands were to be a body politic and corporate.[59] They were to appoint a

Treasurer, who was to perform the duties of a Clerk—to receive and hold for the use of the schools of the township all real estate, personal property, or money conveyed or delivered to him for the use of the schools. The Treasurer was to execute a bond with security which was acceptable to the Trustees.[60]

Divisions 2 and 3 of this act called for the election of a School Commissioner in each county of the state. Their duties were to sell school lands, to collect money from these sales, to loan township funds, and to apply the interest accruing from these funds to the support of the schools. The rate of interest would be twelve percent annually, one-half year paid in advance.

This legislation was an effort on the part of the legislature to curb the selling of school land at wasteful, if not fraudulently-low prices. In Section 24 of this act, the Trustees were directed to divide the land into lots of such size that would bring in the most money. They determined the value and the price for each lot; sales were made to the highest bidder. Section 30 provided that any lot not sold through this procedure could be sold at private sale, but at the value set by the Trustees.

The Commissioner would sell the school land upon the presentation of a petition signed by two-thirds of the white male inhabitants of the township. The regulations for loaning and securing the loan of these funds were set forth in the third division.[61]

Under the School Act of 1841, the powers and duties of the Trustees of School Lands, of the County Commissioners concerning school lands, and of the County School Commissioner, were made to closely parallel those powers and duties long held by Illinois school Trustees and Treasurers.

The fourth division of the act provided for the organization of schools in an unincorporated township. Any number of inhabitants of one or more townships might associate themselves for the purpose of building a school and purchase no more than ten acres of land, to be conveyed to the Trustees of School Lands in the township where the land was situated.[62]

As soon as a school was organized, the employers of teachers were to meet and appoint three of their members as Trustees of the School. At this meeting the employers were to agree upon a plan and manner of conducting the school, and vest the Trustees with the execution of the plan. These Trustees of the School were to visit the schools from time to time to see that the teachers kept regular hours and that the planned schedule was followed.

The Trustees were to continue in service for the duration of the school term, but in no case for more than a year unless reappointed.[63] These Trustees were actually "School Directors."

The interest accruing from township funds and all the profits from use of school lands, and all rents received, were to be applied to the support of the common schools, which were to have been or had been organized according to law.[64]

Thus, in this division of the Act of 1841 is a provision for a school that is to be organized and conducted by the people of a locality or a district, that is separate and aside from the township officialdom, who were given other and specifically different functions by the first three divisions of the act. Also, the three "Trustees of the School" were created to govern and conduct one specific school.

The provisions of the fifth division of the Act of 1841 are of considerable historic interest because they form the basis upon which several schools were formed in the then more-populated areas of Illinois. The special charters for school districts seem to have their foundations here.

The Act of 1841 provided that any congressional township could become incorporated for the purpose of organizing and supporting common schools. Upon written request of ten legal voters in the township, the Trustees of School Lands were to call an election in which all persons entitled to vote for a representative in the General Assembly would be able to vote for or against the proposition.

If the vote was favorable to incorporation, five Trustees were to be elected and were to be known as "Trustees of the Schools" in the township in which they were elected. They were to be successors to the Trustees of School Lands and they were to have and to exercise all rights and powers vested in those Trustees.[65] Their term of office was to be two years and they were to have general superintendence over all the schools in the township. They had the power to lay out the township into districts, suited to the wishes and convenience of the majority of the inhabitants of each district.[66]

The Trustees of Schools were directed to appoint a Treasurer whose duties were generally the same as those prescribed by earlier acts; however, he was given the additional authority to loan the township funds and collect interest therefrom. He was to be governed by the same law as the School Commissioner of the county when dealing with loans. For his renumeration he was paid two percent of the money loaned.[67]

The Trustees of Schools were empowered and directed to examine teachers' qualifications to teach and, if necessary, were to seek assistance of persons qualified to make such examinations.[68]

The latter sections of this act dealt with the incorporated township. Here was the basis for the emergence of Illinois' modern school districts. In each district layed off by the Trustees, the legal voters were directed to meet on the first Saturday in October and select three householders within the district who would be known as "School Directors" and who would continue in office for two years. This board

> . . . had the power to select building places and provide for the building of schools, to furnish them with necessary accomodations, to employ teachers and fix upon their salaries, to visit schools from time to time as well as appoint school visitors, and to make all rules and regulations necessary and proper, and not contrary to law . . . No compensation [was] allowed to School Directors for any service required by this act . . .[69]

These boards were given what at that time was considered the necessary authority to establish and maintain a school. The titles of "Director" and "Trustee" seem ambiguous today and, in all likelihood, were then. Many years afterward, older residents of rural areas referred to the Directors as "Trustees" and students in rural schools recall the Directors, acting in offical capacity, visiting schools during class time.

There have been several important related court decisions involving school officers and school districts. They are quoted, in part:

> School districts and school townships were limited to those powers expressly granted or such as resulted by necessary implications. (People vs. Board of Education of Paris Union School District: 1912, 256, Ill. 568, 99 N.E. 659)[70]

> School officers derive all of their authority from the statute, and must exercise no power not granted and must be governed by provisions of the statutes. (Potter vs. Board of School Trustees, 1882, 10 Ill. App. 343.)[71]

> A school district owned no property, all school facilities, such as grounds, building equipment, etc., were in fact and law property of the State and subject to legislative will. (People vs. Deatherage, 1948, 401 Ill. 25, 81 N.E. 2d. 581.)[72]

In the incorporated townships, the Treasurer was directed to keep separate accounts for each school and to pay the teachers their respective proportions of money received from the School

Commissioner, but not until a report of the number of white children in the district had been filed. The Trustees were to make an apportionment of the interest and profit arising from the township fund as well as the interest arising from the school, college and seminary funds. The money would be distributed according to the number of white children under twenty years of age in each district.[73]

There was also a section in the act which stipulated that "in cases of purchase or dona-

tion of land on which to erect school houses, the conveyance [was to be made] to the Trustees of [the] school . . ."[74]

The Act of 1841 uses, for the first time in Illinois statutes, the term "School Directors." These Directors were to be elected by the legal voters of the district meeting in the "school or another suitable place, on the first Saturday of October. [The directors were] to serve for a term of two years, and they were to be [known as] 'School Directors.' "

## 1843

The school statute in 1843 contained the provision that ". . . a township that had incorporated

could dissolve the corporation by a popular vote."[75]

## 1845

In 1845 the legislature, as it had several times before, repealed practically all school laws; then, the legislature reenacted many of them and also made some startling new enactments.

Probably the most significant provision of the School Act of 1845 was that the Secretary of State was made, ex officio, Superintendent of the Common Schools. In other words, a layman, with perhaps only incidental knowledge of public schools, was made the chief school officer of the state. This law reflects the legislature's feeling that Illinois should have a state system of schools, and as such, should have a State Superintendent. Thomas Campbell, of Jo Daviess County, the incumbent Secretary of State, became the first Superintendent of Schools, later to be called the Superintendent of Public Instruction.

The Law of 1845 placed overwhelming, if not impossible, responsibilities upon the Superinten-

dent. Although untrained in education, he was required by law to supervise all common schools of the state and to act as the general advisor and assistant to the County School Commissioners. He was to recommend the most approved textbooks, charts, and apparatus, and, furthermore, was to urge uniformity in the use of each.[76]

According to some accounts of Mr. Campbell's administration, considerable pressure was exerted on him by teachers and their friends in an effort to soften the effects of a new law which raised the standards of qualifications for teachers. The law would have forced ineffective teachers to retire; some historians feel that it is to Mr. Campbell's credit that he held strictly to this controversial law.[77]

The Act of 1845 also made the County School Commissioner, ex officio, Superintendent of the common schools fo the county and gave him the responsibility of examining all teachers' qualifications to teach orthography, reading in English, penmanship, arithmetic, English grammar, modern geography, and U.S. history. He was permitted to employ capable associates for these examinations. The teachers who fulfilled these requirements were to be given certificates of qualification. Without a certificate, no person could be paid out of public funds.[78] Thus, by this action, the Trustees were relieved of the responsibility of examining teachers.

Another stipulation of the Act of 1845 stated that when the County Commissioners loaned funds of their office, eight percent interest per year was to be charged, one-half year to be paid in advance.[79]

The act also gave the Commissioners and the Trustees of schools in unincorporated townships the authority to purchase real estate if, in their opinion, the interest of the fund would be promoted.[60]

The School Act of 1845 also created the school township. The school township differs from a congressional township (created in 1785) in that, while the boundaries are generally the same, the school township may include, in some cases, a fractional congressional township which has been attached to a neighboring school township.[81]

Three Trustees were to be elected by the voters of each incorporated township, for a two year term, and their corporate body was to be known as "Trustees of township _____ range _____.[82] In succeeding elections, the corporate body of the Trustees was to be known as "Trustees of Schools" of the township in which they were elected.[83] The Trustees were to be successors to the Trustees of School Lands and Trustees of Schools, which were elected through the authority of the Common School Act of 1841, now repealed almost in totum by the Act of 1845.[84] The Trustees were to appoint to a two-year term a Treasurer "who might or might not have been from their number." The Treasurer retained many of his original duties, except, by this act, he was made, ex officio, Superintendent of all the common schools of the township. He was to visit schools from time to time, was to confer with School Directors and teachers, and was to communicate to them the plans and suggestions of County and State Superintendents, using his influence to carry out such plans.[85] He was also to furnish the School Commissioner such information concerning the township schools as the Commissioner was required to communicate to the State Superintendent.[86]

The Treasurer continued to be the sole legal custodian of the funds of the incorporated township and was directed to keep the funds, and any interest not paid to the teachers, to be loaned at interest. If the Trustees wished, however, the funds could be kept by the School Commissioner who could loan them at interest.[87]

The Act of 1845 also shows that for the first time in Illinois, a school was required to use textbooks printed in the English language, and that English had to be the common medium of communication in the school, if that school desired any benefit from the public or town fund.[88]

In this act, the legislature made strides toward establishing some state assistance to the schools. It provided that 6% interest on the Common School Fund and the College and Seminary Fund should be apportioned and paid to the various counties, and, by them, to the townships, on the basis of the number of white children under the age of twenty-one years of age in the counties. (One section of a former statute directed apportionment on the basis of the number under twenty years. Which age was used as a determiner is unknown.) A program of schedules was made by the teachers and reported to the Auditor; this was the basis of apportionment. The system, in some ways, resembles Illinois' present system; the number of payments actually made by the state is unknown.[89]

The Act of 1845 also gave teachers the right to bring suit against Trustees if and when they felt they were not receiving their portion of the distributive fund.[90]

School Commissioners were allowed three percent on the returns from the sale of school lands and two percent on money loaned from the township fund. School Treasurers were to receive two percent on loans and reloans, but only when the money was collected from one person and loaned to another.[91]

Criminal actions were to be instituted against any School Commissioner, Trustee or Treasurer when charged with misuse of funds or attempts to defraud the state or any local school fund. Trustees were liable for the sufficiency of Treasurers' bonds.[92]

Because of its uniqueness, Section 87 is quoted here in full:

> No justice of the peace, constable, clerk of a court, or sheriff, shall charge any cost in any suit where any agent of any school fund suing for recovery of the same, or any interest due thereon, is plaintiff, and shall be, from any cause, unsuccessful in such suit.[93]

Because of its importance, the School Act of 1845 is offered in summation: (1) it made the Secretary of State the first chief state school officer; (2) it made the County School Commissioner, ex officio, the County Superintendent of the Township Schools; (3) it provided that the Treasurer might also be one of the Trustees; (4) it returned to the Treasurer the authority and responsibility to loan school funds; (5) it gave the County Commissioner the duty of examining teacher qualifications; (6) it made English the language of the school system and its texts; (7) it gave teachers legal recourse concerning payment of school funds; (8) it stiffened laws against fraud and willful mismanagement of school funds; and (9) it began a sophisticated system, based upon student schedules, for the distribution of state funds.

Several court decisions which deal with congressional townships are cited from Smith-Hurd Annotated Statutes:

> There [were] no constitutional limitations placed on the legislature as to the agencies the state should adopt for providing for free schools. *People ex rel. Brockamp vs. Chicago & I.M. Ry. Co., 1913, 256 Ill. 488, 100 N.E. 174.*
> *Legislature could create or divide school townships or school funds [at] its discretion. People vs. Board of Education of Paris Union School District, 1912; 255 Ill. 568, 99 N.E. 659.*[94]

# 1847

The School Act of 1847 consisted of 120 sections. Technically, it repealed all provisions of the Acts of 1841 and 1845; realistically, it simply rewrote and revised these and other former acts. Section 121 provided that the public printer print ten thousand copies of the act and specified the manner of distribution for its use by various "officers [affected by the] law."[95]

According to Section 33, the inhabitants of a township, if they chose, could "adopt the School Commissioner to be in place of and discharge

27

the duties of the Trustees of Schools in matters of keeping and loaning school funds for the township." In such a case, he would be governed by the same law as the Trustees and Township Treasurers.[96] Another provision was "that districts [could] be altered at any time by the Trustees [in order] to suit the wishes of a majority of the inhabitants in the district."[97]

The usual three Trustees were to be elected by the voters of the township and were to be known as "Trustees of Schools, of township _____ range _____." They were successors to the Trustees of School Lands, and Trustees of Schools, provided by the Acts of 1841 and 1845.[98] Upon election, the Trustees were to appoint a Treasurer, who was *not* to be one of their number.[99]

By this act the Township Treasurer was given full authority over loaning township funds, according to law. Interest was to be eight percent, one-half year payable in advance. Trustees were to meet quarterly and proceed to apportion to each district its share of the interest from the school, college and seminary funds, and the rents, interest, etc. from the township funds. The apportioned share was to be paid to the various District Treasurers.[100] This is the first statutory mention of District Treasurers: ". . . Upon their election, . . . [the] School Directors [were to] agree upon and appoint one of their number Treasurer, to be called the District Treasurer."[101]

The acts of 1845[102] and 1847[103] provided for a meeting of the "inhabitants, the legal voters" of the district to decide whether or not to tax themselves for building and furnishing a school and supporting their schools. First, they voted to determine if a tax for these purposes should be levied; a two-thirds favorable vote was required. After the vote they were to agree upon a rate, not to exceed fifteen cents on the one hundred dollars.

The Act of 1847 further provided that a levy, not to exceed fifty cents, could be authorized to purchase a lot or to build or furnish a building for school purposes.

## 1847

The 1849 legislature made few changes in laws dealing with School Trustees and Treasurers except that ten percent interest was charged on loans. Three Trustees were still required by law, but they were directed to meet "half-yearly" instead of quarterly, as before.[104] The Township Treasurer continued to be the ex officio Superintendent of Schools of the township.

In its dealings with the local schools, however, the General Assembly was considerably more friendly. By revised terms, the annual meeting to determine a tax levy required only a simple majority of those voting in order to make a levy. For general school purposes the rate could go to twenty-five cents on the hundred dollars, instead of fifteen, as before; the building levy could go to five hundred dollars.[105]

Due to the increase in population, the public printer was directed to print 15,000 copies of the Act of 1849 to be distributed throughout the state.[106]

The School Act of 1855 was one of the most important pieces of legislation affecting public education in Illinois. Many historians feel that this is when the methods of financing schools finally came of age. Prior to 1855, as has been stated, the people of Illinois and their elected officials had been willing to use any means possible to derive funds for running expenses of government, including the Common School Fund, short of reaching down into their pockets and paying the necessary amount in taxes.

The General Assembly changed all this, however, with the School Act of 1855 which revolutionized support of the common schools of the state.

One section provided that the state would levy a tax of two mills on each dollar of valuation of all taxable property in the state. The sum raised was to be placed in the Common School Fund of the State, along with other monies from other sources, heretofore provided, to be distributed to the common schools of the state.[107]

Further, the Board of Township Trustees was directed to estimate the total sum needed, in addition to the State School Fund, to operate the schools of their township; a tax rate was then to be levied on the property of the township and to be collected, sufficient to raise this sum.[108]

For the purpose of purchasing school sites, erecting schools, purchasing furniture, fuel, and district libraries, the boards of directors were authorized to have levied and collected a tax annually on all taxable property in the district.[109]

Finally, the act conferred on school directors the power to borrow money through the sale of bonds in sums of not less than $100. The money was to be used to purchase school sites, and to erect, repair, and improve schools. The interest rate was not to exceed ten percent per year, and the sum thus borrowed was not to exceed one percent of the value of the property in the district.[110]

Prior to passing this act, the General Assembly had taken an important step toward upgrading the state school system, when, in a special session called by Governor Matteson in 1854, it established the State Superintendent of Schools as an elective office with a term of two years and a salary of $1,500 per year.[111]

By this action, the people were given the opportunity to choose for their chief school officer one who had sole duty for superintending the schools and who had some special knowledge of schools.

In 1865, the State Superintendent's term was lengthened to four years and the salary was raised to $2,500.[112]

As discussed earlier, in 845 the County School Commissioners were made, ex officio, County Superintendents of Schools, relegating the educational functions of the office secondary to those of land administration; in 1855, the General Assembly made this office the County Superintendent of Schools, who was to be elected on the first Monday in November, every two years, as was the case in the election and length of term of the State Superintendent of Public Instruction.

This position retained the usual duties of examining and certifying teachers, visiting schools (for which he was to received two dollars per day, not to exceed forty days), and receiving and transmitting reports on the condition of the county's schools to the State Superintendent. To the position were added the following powers and duties relating to the School Trustees and the Township School Treasurers:

1. Enjoined to keep three books (A, B, and C) as records of school lands, mortgages, etc.

2. Empowered to receive bonds of Township School Treasurers.

3. Directed to apportion state school funds.

4. Provided that he should loan the principal, but not the interest, of county and township funds.

5. Directed and empowered him to sell and resell real estate.

6. Allowed the County Superintendent to receive the usual three and two percent fees on land sold and funds loaned.

7. Empowered the Superintendent to hire competent personnel to secure and compile statistics when Trustees fail to do so, these persons to be paid out of township funds.[113]

The Board of Trustees, as usual, was directed to appoint a Township Treasurer, who should not be one of their number, nor should he be a Director; the Treasurer was to be Clerk of the Board of Trustees. The Treasurer was required to execute a bond, with two or more freeholders as sureties, who should not be a member of a board of education.[114]

Prior to 1855, one of the Trustees was appointed to preside at each meeting, but in this year the law required that they elect one of their members as President, who like the Treasurer, was to serve as such during the term for which the appointing Trustees had been elected.[115]

The Treasurer was obliged to loan all money which came into his hands by virtue of his office, except that which was subject to distribution to the schools; interest on all loans was to be at the rate of ten percent, payable half year in advance. These loans were not to be made for less than six months nor more than five years.[116]

# 1857 & 1861

In an amendment to the school law in 1857 the legislature directed the Township Trustees to "lay off the township into districts to suit the wishes and convenience of the majority of the inhabitants of the township."[117] The obvious purpose of the provision was to make schools conveniently available to all children in the township. In 1861, the legislature, perhaps acted out of dissatisfaction with the non-compliance of some Boards of Trustees with this provision, as evidenced by the Preamble and Provisions of an act passed in that year:

> Whereas section thirty-three of 'an act to establish and maintain a system of free schools, approved February 16, 1857; makes it the duty of school trustees in the several organized townships . . . to divide their respective townships into two or more school districts; and whereas some of the townships have been organized into one district, and a tax for school purposes has been levied by the corporate authorities thereof on the whole pro-perty of the township to erect a school-house or support a school in one extreme part thereof; therefore: . . . all school taxes levied by the corporate authorities of any township or school district, in townships not divided into two or more school districts, are hereby declared illegal and void.[118]

Further, the act provided that no school tax whatsoever should be levied or collected on property that did not lie within three miles of a school.[119]

This Act of 1861 was undoubtedly a stern reprimand to Trustees who had not followed the provisions of the former act; further, it set the pattern which courts have followed many times since, in which they stated that schools should be as convenient as is reasonably possible to most students.

The Act of 1857 also provided that before apportionment of funds was made to the districts on their schedules, there should be deducted such amount as the Directors had requested be set aside for support of schools in the summer.[120] Even in the early years of the Twentieth Century, the school year consisted of two sessions, winter and spring (or summer) "terms," in most rural districts.

The Board of Trustees, in their corporate capacity, were invested with the title, care, and custody of all schools and school sites; the supervision and control of them were expressly vested in school districts where the property was located.[121] This provision indicates a further erosion of the authority of Trustees and an increase in the authority of School Directors.

One amendment in the School Act of 1857 has had impact on school lands since its inception.

Even in recent years there have been frequent controversies over rural school sites which were either land granted to the Trustees for school purposes only, or were obtained by eminent domain. What follows is one of several passages referring to the Act of 1857.

Under Laws 1857, where school trustees took title to school site by eminent domain with owner's consent, the title of the School Trustees was the statutory title granted by the legislature, and where there was no evidence that school trustees procured any other kind of title, or that they ever made any claim to any other kind of title, they could by their acts obtain only such title as was necessary for the conduct of school, (Superior Oil Co. vs. Harsh, D.C. 1941. 39 F. Supp. 467. affirmed 126 F. 2d. 572)[122]

## 1859

Two acts passed by the 1859 General Assembly deserve mention. The first provision in the law permitted two or more school districts, either in one township or in more, to consolidate, and set up the machinery for such act, which was handled by the Trustees.[123] The other act dealt with the length of the school term. It was provided that the Directors should ascertain the amount of money needed to support "free schools for six months," further establishing guidelines for the length of time which schools should operate.[124]

## 1861-1864

As might be expected, there was little important action on school law involving Trustees and Treasurers during the period of the Civil War. The Act in 1861, reprimanding negligent School Trustees, was mentioned under this study's treatment of the 1857 school legislation. 1863 saw no legislative action which directly affected School Trustees and Treasurers.

## 1865

There was no significant change in the laws affecting School Trustees from 1845-1865. In 1865, the term of office of Trustees was increased to three years.[125]

In addition, Treasurers were directed to loan all money, except that portion which was to be distributed, for not less than six percent interest nor more than ten percent per year, one-half to be paid in advance.[126]

## 1869

The school law was amended in 1869 to provide that Trustees should be elected annually on the second Monday in April. The exception provided was that in counties under township organizations, where the boundaries of the school and civil townships were identical, the Trustees should be elected in the same election as other township officers, namely, the day of the annual town meeting.[127]

## 1871-1872

The inception of a new constitution in 1870 created many changes in the form and the content of the law. Private laws were prohibited; concerning school law, this meant no more special charters and no more private laws relating to a particular district or area, except by general class. Classifications based upon population were acceptable, provided the classification was reasonable. This meant that classification by population would not be legal in cases where population was no factor. The school code was completely revised in 1871. "The real basis for the present law came in 1872 when former legislation was incorporated into law and fractional townships were permitted to be consolidated."[128]

When such fractional townships contained less than forty persons under twenty-one years of age, the Trustees, when petitioned by a majority of the inhabitants, were permitted to enter into a written agreement with the Board of Trustees of an adjacent township to consolidate territory, school funds, and other property, all of which were to be managed by the Board of Trustees of the adjacent and consolidated township. The Board of Trustees of the fractional township would then cease to exercise the functions of School Trustees of the fractional township.[129]

For the first time, legislation permitted voters of a township to vote for or against establishing and maintaining a township high school. For quite some time, there had been considerable pressure to adopt the "township system" instead of the established district system of school organization. The aforesaid provision appears to have been a result of that pressure. The Trustees were to accept a petition of the voters of the township, were to call the election, and were to handle the details and machinery of transaction.[130]

This provision was further amended in 1879, to provide that having established such a township high school, the voters might discontinue it if a proposition to discontinue received a favorable vote in an election held for that purpose. Such an election was to be called for by a petition signed by a majority of legal voters of the township. The Trustees were directed to call the election to discontinue, and if the proposition prevailed, they were to distribute the assets of the district so discontinued.[131] Furthermore, in 1889, two or more townships were permitted to cooperate in forming a township high school, in the manner explained above, "on such terms as they may," by written agreement made and signed by the Boards of Trustees, enter into.[132]

Undoubtedly, there was considerable controversy over the division of newly organized territory into school districts. To deal with this controversy, the legislature (in 1871-72) gave the inhabitants of a township a choice of five different conditions for drawing up a petition to be presented to the Board of Trustees upon which the division should be made; the division should be thus made, "and not otherwise."[133]

In 1877, an amendatory sixth provision was added giving the Board of Trustees discretionary powers in changing district boundaries and creating new districts when petitioned, as previously explained. Further, an opportunity to appeal of the Board of Trustees a decision to the County Superintendent was provided.[134]

The Act of 1871 also made a change in the required report made by the Board of Trustees to the County Superintendent. The change required, that in addition to the usual statistics, the Board's report should include an "enumeration of those persons above the age of twelve years who [were] unable to read and write . . ." Furthermore, the report was to fix ". . . the cause or causes of this failure to educate."[135]

Another change created by the Act of 1871 was in the date of the election of Township Trustees. The new date was the second Saturday in April, with the same provision for election in concurrent school and civil townships as was included in the law of 1869.[136]

In several preceding acts, the Board of Trustees was directed to turn over to the Township Treasurer all money for the use of the township and districts. Not until 1871 did the law expressly provide that "the Township Treasurer . . . [was] declared to be the only lawful depository and custodian of all township and district funds."[137]

There was also an amendment made to the election code, providing that no "spiritous, malt, vinous, or intoxicating liquor could be sold or given away within one mile of a place holding any general or special election on election day;" this was interpreted to include school elections.[138]

The interest on public funds loaned by the Township Treasurer should be not less than 8 percent annually, and not more than 10 percent, one-half to be paid in advance. Interest on delinquent loans was to be 12 percent.[139]

## 1877

Except for the amendatory action mentioned above which affected boundary changes, there were few changes created by the law in 1877. A sentence was added to the section on Trustee eligibility, providing that when there were three or more school districts in any one township, no two Trustees could reside, when elected, in the same school district.[140]

Women were given the right to hold, by appointment or election, any school office for which they had the same qualifications, for the office, as any man.[141]

As explained, in 1859 the Directors of School were directed to ascertain the amount of money needed to finance the schools of their districts for a six-month period. In 1871 this period was changed to "not less than five months nor more than nine."[142]

In 1877, the school code was put in Chapter 122 of the Revised Statutes.

## 1879

As mentioned above, the law of 1879 marked the first time that the provision to discontinue the township high school appeared in school law.

One other provision in this act reduced the interest rate the Treasurer should charge on money loaned. The old rate was "not less than eight and not more than ten percent, annually, one-half year in advance." The new rate was reduced to "not less than six and not more than eight percent, annually." The "one-half year in advance" clause was omitted.[143] This change no doubt reflected the changing economic conditions of the state.

## 1883

In 1883, the legislature once again showed its concern for the large sums of money lying idle in the treasuries of some special charter districts. This was due to the fact that charters required the high interest rate prevailing on the date of the issuance of the charter. The 1883 legislature gave those districts the right to loan their money at the "rate set by law, now and hereinafter provided."[144]

The act of 1883 set the term of the President of the Board of Trustees at one year and it remained so until 1929 when it was increased to two years. The term of the Treasurer was set at two years.[145]

## 1887

1887 brought extensive changes in the sections of the law dealing with district boundary change; these changes seem more significant in their import than in their magnitude or substance and seem to reflect the growing tendency in Illinois to consider school district lines sacrosanct and almost beyond change. This attitude caused Illinois to cling to an ancient school district system, which, ignoring economy and educational opportunity for many students, built up to nearly 12,000 districts, lasting until almost the middle of the Twentieth Century.

# 1889

The entire school code seems to have been rewritten in 1889. The sections were renumbered; they were also divided, making them shorter and easier to read. For example, Section 33 had been a single paragraph, three and one-half pages long; it was most difficult to read and comprehend. The main purpose of the revision was to eliminate passages of this type.

In 1889, the code was arranged into sixteen different articles, each dealing with a single subject; a more readable and usable code was the result. Even with all this change in form, however, there seems to have been little change in content.

The population growth in some areas of the state was acknowledged by the inclusion of a provision in the election of Trustees, that there should be one polling place for each eight hundred legal voters in the township.[146] Further legislation dictated that no person could be a Trustee and a School Director at the same time.[147]

In 1879, women were given the right to hold any office, elective or appointed, chosen under the school law; in 1891 women were given the right to vote in any election held for the purpose of choosing any officers of schools under general or special school laws of the state.[148] Apparently, since the right was extended only to election of officers, women were not, by this act, entitled to vote on any other school propositions.

The section of the school code dealing with boundary change through petition and with election in districts of less than one thousand population was amended to include special charter districts.[149]

*Smith-Hurd Annotated Statutes* cites a decision in a case arising from the above section:

> Under prior law, if election of school trustees was held under provisions of school law Australian Ballot Act, Laws of 1891, Page 107, sec. 1 . . . did not apply, while it did apply if trustees were elected at the same election as township officers. People vs. Brown, 1901, 189, Ill. 60 N.E. 46.[150]

# 1899

There were no changes in the laws affecting Trustees in the 1899 session of the General Assembly; only one change was made which affected Treasurers. The interest rate charged on loans was to be not less than five percent nor more than seven percent annually. For all sums not exceeding $200 and for a time less than one year, responsible sureties were required; for sums over $200 and for longer than one year, security was to be a mortgage on unincumbered real estate worth at least 40% more than the amount loaned.[151]

## 1905

In 1905, the interest was reduced to not less than four percent and not more than seven percent, annually, on money loaned by the Treasurer.[152] It remained at that figure until 1943, when it was set at not less than four percent.

## 1909

The school law was revised in 1909, but as in 1889, most of the change was in form rather than in content. The law was organized more coherently and was revised to eliminate wordiness.

An amendment in 1909 provided for a minimum of two polling places for the election of Trustees; it also provided that one of the Trustees should be assigned to each polling place and that additional judges should be chosen from the voters present. There was to be one polling place for each 800 voters. The amendment of 1929 incorporated the provisions of this section in its present form.[153]

The provision outlining the appointment of the Treasurer by the Trustee was clearly stated:

"within ten days after election of Trustees in 1910, and biennially thereafter, the Trustees shall elect a treasurer."[154]

The loan section of the school code was changed to read, in part, that

... no loan shall be made for less than one year nor more than five years. All loans shall be secured by unincumbered real estate located in [Illinois], valued at at least 50% more than the amount loaned, with a condition that in case additional security shall be required at any time it shall be given to the satisfaction of the Trustees of School.[155]

## 1929

An amendment in 1929 increased the term of office of Trustees to six years; they were to be elected in odd numbered years.[156] Townships formed from two or more congressional townships were to be considered school townships and Trustees were to be elected at the same time and in the same manner, and with the same powers, rights, and duties as other Township Trustees.[157] The Law of 1929 also brought about an increase in the term of office of President of the Board of Trustees to two years.[158]

## 1935

In 1935, the Treasurers were authorized to invest township funds in bonds or debentures of various specified corporations formed to purchase federally guaranteed mortgages under the Federal Housing Administrator, and to exchange mortgages in default for bonds of the Home Owners Loan Corporation.[159]

House Bill 170 in 1935 called for the abolition of Township Treasurers. Instead, House Bill 170 called for the Trustees to appoint a clerk, who was neither a Trustee nor a Director, who would perform the duties of the Treasurer. The bill was not enacted.[160]

## 1937

1937 was a bad financial year for many school districts. This was reflected in a proposed-but-defeated measure that would have required that orders issued by the Township Treasurer show on the face the numerical order of issue; the

Treasurer would have notified the Clerk of the School Board, who would have then notified the teacher that funds were available to pay the order.[161]

## 1939

The law which required high school districts to pay a part of the salary of the Township Treasurer was amended so that the part each should pay would be determined by dividing the total

amount of funds handled by the Treasurer by the amount of the funds belonging to each high school district.[162]

## 1941

According to the school code passed in 1941, the Township Treasurer was permitted to file a bond approved by a surety company authorized to do business in Illinois.[163] Another amendment provided that if individuals were sureties on the bond required to be filed by the Treasurer, that it should be for not less than one and one-half

times the largest amount estimated as coming into his hands, nor less than the largest amount estimated by such governing body if the surety was a surety company authorized to do business in Illinois.[164]

## 1943

1943 brought only a few changes in the school code. The Township Trustees were directed to enter upon their duties on the twentieth day after their election.[165] An unrelated law set the interest rate on loans by the Treasurer at not less than four percent annually.

The section of the code which required a statement of condition of funds was amended to provide that within 90 days of July 1, annually, a financial statement for the township and each school district therein had to be included in the Trustee's annual report submitted to the County Superintendent. This statement was to be published in a newspaper of general circulation in the township. By no later than October 15, the Treasurer was to present to the County Superintendent a certified statement that the publication had been made and he was also required to present them with a copy of the newspaper containing the publication; funds could be withheld from the Treasurer if he did not comply.[166] A more in-depth examination of this amendment is in *Smith-Hurd Annotated Statutes,* 1961, page 309, Historical Note.

## 1945-1959
## Years of Consolidation

## 1945

The school code was revised again in 1945. There were many changes in form and language, but no substantive changes in content. However, most, if not all, of the bills that were passed amending the code before it was sent on to the governor for approval. Two of those related to Trustees and Treasurers.

The "payment of claims" section was amended to provide that an insufficiency in income from the permanent fund could be supplemented by taking the additional amount needed from the total of other funds. The claims to be met included: (1) compensation of the Treasurer, (2) the publication cost for the annual statement, (3) the cost of the record book, if any, and (4) the cost of dividing school land and of making plats.[167] (In 1953, this was further amended to read: "each district [is to be] charged as its share . . . the proportion which the amount of school funds of the district handled by the Treasure bears to the total amount of school funds handled by that Treasurer.")[168]

Also, it was provided that a vacancy on the Board of Trustees would be filled within thirty days, by the remaining Trustees, until the next regular election.[169]

## 1949

Only one act was passed and approved in the 1949 session which directly affected Township Trustees and Treasurers. According to this new law, when there was no property in a school district not subject to taxation for ordinary operating purposes, the Trustees of the township wherein the district is located would apportion the assets of the district among the other districts of the township according to the last preceding apportionment from the Common School Fund.[170]

One bill in 1949 called for the establishment of a commission to study the functions of the Township Trustees and Treasurers. This bill advocated replacement of the Trustees and Treasurers by a County Board of Education to assume the functions performed by the Trustees and a single County Officer to assume the functions performed by the Treasurers. The measure failed to pass the Senate.[171]

## 1951

From 1819 to 1950, the general pattern of school townships and their officers, Trustees and Treasurers, changed very little, except for an increase in number as more townships were organized. In the 1948-49 school year, for example, 1,755 Treasurers filed reports.

During this same period, the number of school districts rose from none to 11,955 by the year 1945. The first School Problems Commission, in its report filed in 1951, stated: "The most striking change that has occurred in Illinois school matters has been the reduction, since 1945, in the number of school districts . . . from a total of 11,955 to, as of September 1, 1950, a total of 4,580, a reduction of 7,375."[172] Most of the districts eliminated were rural districts with tiny, one-room schools, located, generally, every two miles apart. There were, on the average, slightly more than six districts per township throughout the state.

Printed below is a passage taken from the School Problems Commission's report:

It may be granted that the school township in Illinois served a useful purpose and operated effectively a century ago. It is closely related to the district system of organization and especially the creation of small, rural, elementary schools. That it has become obsolete and in need of sharp modification has been recognized for over three decades and was vigorously pointed out to the School Problems Commission at all its public hearings this year. The transfer of its financial functions was recommended by the Report of the Efficiency and Economy Committee of 1915, by the Griffenhafen report to the Illinois Commission on Taxation and Expenditures, in 1932, by the report of the Illinois Agricultural Association School Commission in 1944, and by many other agencies.

Meanwhile, the school township organization has persisted although the reorganization of school districts has made its functioning more troublesome and inefficient than ever. The School Problems Commission heard from 18 persons concerning the problem of the school township. All of them advocated some change in the present system. No one has come before the Commission to support the present school township or to oppose its modification.[173]

Data from the same report indicates that of the 1,755 Township Treasurers who reported in 1948-49, 538 were inactive; they had no legal responsibility other than taking care of the loanable fund. In twenty-six counties across central Illinois there were as many (or more) inactive Treasurers as active.[174]

The report stated that this data revealed ". . . the absurdity of the system [when compared to] the creation of larger districts. With many districts including complete townships, it is unlikely that many of these Treasurers will ever become active again."[175] Scott County, for example, a county unit (a single school district in the entire county) had ten Treasurers, nine of which were "inactive." One of these "inactive" Treasurers had an income from the loanable fund of $105 in 1848-49, while the expenses of his office were $128.[176] Jersey County had thirteen school townships and thirteen School Treasurers, although it had only one school district.[177]

It is safe to say that hundreds of "inactive" Treasurers were caught in a mesh of legal requirements that they be bonded and that they publish a report of a job that did nothing worthwhile and which neither they nor anyone else wanted.

Meanwhile, the active as well as the inactive Treasurers continued to manage the loanable fund (including school lands). In 1948-49, the total amount of loanable funds in the entire state, exclusive of Chicago, was $6,661,924, or an average of less than $3,800 per Treasurer. (Chicago is excluded because it is not organized as a township, and the City Treasurer is Custodian of the School Fund.) In only four counties—Cook, Ford, Livingston, and McLean—does the fund total as much as $250,000.[178]

A table in the report documents the very great growth in the expense of the office of Township School Treasurers during the years from 1930 to 1949, and the decline in the income of the loanable fund for the same period. "The result," says the report, "has been the alarming increase in the excess of expense over income, a deficiency that must be paid for from the state distributive fund. This excess has risen from $8,809 in 1930 to $721,445 in 1949."[179]

The Commission concluded that (1) many treasurers were not needed, (2) the loanable fund, including school lands, was a trifling amount in most counties, and (3) that the yield of the loanable fund did not begin to cover the cost of the Treasurers' office.[180] It is apparent that the Commission felt the cost of the office made this a state problem to be dealt with by the legislature.

There are nine types of duties for the School Trustees and Treasurers, but the Commission felt only three were of any importance: (1) those connected with the loanable fund, (2) those giving custody of other funds, and (3) those affecting a change in school district boundary lines. In making its recommendations concerning the first type of duty, the Commission revealed the median expense of running the office of Treasurer was $361 while the median income from the office was but $39; it concluded that "So far as 'inactive' Treasurers [were] concerned, the system [was] expensive, useless, ridiculous, and in many ways detrimental."[181] When studying the second type of duty, the Commission stated that one full time County School Treasurer could handle the duties of all Township Treasurers in each county, thus creating a savings of $188,000 per year; it was possible in many counties for a part-time clerk to handle the work, thereby effecting a much larger saving. In deciding upon the third type of duty, the Commission reasoned that since Township Trustees' authority did not reach beyond their own township, boundary changes were more properly a state or county function.[182]

In order to secure a more suitable plan for handling the township school problems, the Commission made the following recommendations to the 67th General Assembly which was due to meet in January of 1951:

(a) That a seven member, non-salaried Board of School Trustees be elected in the primary election to replace the Township Trustees, effective July 1, 1952.

(b) That the County Board of School Trustees act in district boundary changes. (Special charter districts were exempt from this provision.)

(c) That the County Board of School Trustees hold title to and manage all permanent funds and common school lands. Permanent funds of less than $10,000 would be liquidated and those over that amount could be retained, with provision to be made to handle them.

(d) That custody of school funds be transferred to School Treasurers or to the County Superintendent of Schools. The County Superintendent would be ex-officio Treasurer of all districts except special charter districts and districts of over 5,000 population who would have the privilege of appointing their own Treasurer.

(e) That the transfer of duties from the Township Treasurer to the County Superintendent and from the Township Trustees to the County Board of School Trustees be carefully provided by law.[183]

A more-thorough explanation of the township school problems can be found in pages 16 through 19 and all of Chapter 8 of the Report of the School Problems Commission.

Even though the legislature did not immediately accept all of these recommendations by the School Problems Commission, it did, within the next ten years or so, enact most if not all of those necessary for a modern and efficient system of school management. The progress made in subsequent sessions, however, was based upon the facts and conditions cited by this Commission. There was not complete unanimity among the Commission members in support of the recommendations; one legislative member and one member at large dissented from most of them.

Eight bills were introduced in the 67th General Assembly in 1951 to implement the Commission's recommendations: House Bills 825, 826, 827, 830, 1190, 1191, and 1193. Only three substantive bills in this group were

enacted into law at this session: 825, which created the County Board of School Trustees; 1190, which removed authority for boundary changes from the Township Trustees; and 835, which placed this authority with the County Board of School Trustees.[184]

The bill, which created the County Board of School Trustees followed the Commission's recommendations for structure and organization. The County Board was to consist of seven non-salaried members who would serve for a six-year term; the County Superintendent of Schools would serve as Secretary of the Board. This Board would have authority to act on all school district boundary changes. Thus, Township Trustees were relieved completely of any authority over changing district lines; this was the first important change in their authority governing lands since 1872 when the power to initiate such changes was taken from them and given to Boards of School Directors and School Boards. All other powers formerly held by the Township Trustees were retained by them.[185]

House Bill 1165 was introduced very late in the session; it would have provided for the continuance of Township Trustees in Cook County. Since the bill to abolish them did not pass, House Bill 1165 was tabled as unnecessary.

An amendment to the Treasurer's bond section of the school code provided that the penalty of the bond should be twice the amount of all bonds, notes, mortgages, and money if individuals acted as sureties, or an amount equal to all such effects if the surety was a surety company; it was to be increased or decreased from time to time when it was the judgment of the County Superintendent of Schools or the Trustees that the penalty should be increased or decreased.[186]

# 1953

In a report to the 68th General Assembly in March of 1953, the School Problems Commission #2 again recommended that the office of Township Trustees and Treasurers be eliminated; it further stated: "Such legislation should not apply to Cook County, where, because of the number of populous districts and the complexity of finance matters . . . the existing system should be continued."[187] To have applied the same treatment to Cook County as was recommended for the balance of the state would have increased the number of Treasurers. The Commission felt that this would have been undesirable. It was further proposed that the "counties should be divided into two classes: one consisting of Cook, and the other [consisting of] the downstate counties."[188]

This Second Commission further recommended that the duties of the Township Trustees in all counties except Cook be transferred to the County Board of School Trustees and that Township Treasurers, except in Cook, be abolished and that the County Superintendent of Schools be named Treasurer ex officio of all school districts in the county. It was recommended, however, that districts having a population of at least 5,000, and unit districts having a population of at least 2,000, should be able to appoint their own Treasurer if they so desire.[189]

Regardless, the cost of the Treasurer was to be borne by the district; the County Superintendent was to pro rate the cost of administering these duties to the various districts. No trustees were to be elected in April of 1954.[190]

Finally, the Commission recommended that small loanable funs be liquidated and that Township Fund Commissioners should be established to administer those funds which were sufficient to provide an income of $2,500 annually.[191]

To comply with these recommendations, the 68th General Assembly introduced three bills.

House Bill 757 was the most important bill in this series. The Commission's recommendation and the Bill's original form stated that only Cook County should be classified as a Class II county, thereby retaining its Township Trustees and Treasurers. In its final form, the bill was amended to include as Class II counties any county with a population over 180,000, thereby including Madison and St. Clair. The bill went into effect on July 1, 1954; there were to be no more elected Township Trustees in ninety-eight counties of Illinois and there were to be no more appointed Township School Treasurers.

House Bill 757 also provided that all permanent funds in areas where income was less than $2,500 per year would be liquidated by the County Board of School Trustees; after expenses had been paid, the balance would be distributed to the schools of the township under other provisions of the act. Where the permanent fund produced an income of $2,500 or more annually, three Township Land Commissioners were to be elected by the voters of the township; these commissioners were to manage the school lands and the permanent fund.[192]

This bill provided that in Class I counties (all except the three named previously) each School Board was to appoint its own Treasurer; however, three-member boards were to appoint a person who was Treasurer in a district governed by a seven-member board.[193]

Two other bills were passed in 1953 which affected Trustees and Treasurers. House Bills 756 and 758 were supportive of the provisions of 757 and brought other sections of the law in compliance with it.[194]

Historians and scholars agree that some long-overdue changes were made in school organization in this and the previous session of the General Assembly and that real progress toward modernization of the school system had been effected.

In 1953 and for several years thereafter, the statutes relating to Township Trustees and Treasurers were revised to conform to the General Revision Act of 1951.

## 1955

In 1955, the School Problems Commission made no recommendations which directly affected Township Trustees and Treasurers, nor did the General Assembly pass legislation directly affecting Trustees and Treasurers.

Two bills were introduced by non-Commission members, but the bills were not enacted. One of the bills would have abolished Trustees and Treasurers in Class II counties. The bill was not called for action. The other bill would have directed the Trustees to appoint one of their members as Treasurer. The bill passed the House, but was tabled in the Senate.[195]

The increasing concentration of population in the urban areas of the state was responsible for the only substantive change in the law which would effect Trustees or Treasurers. The change provided that when 90% or more of the electors of a township resided in one school district, the following restriction should be removed: "not more than one Trustee could reside in the same school district, when elected."[196]

## 1957

In 1957, the School Problem Commission once again recommended the abolition of Trustees and Treasurers in Madison and St. Clair Counties; since there seemed to be little chance of passing such legislation, no bill to accomplish this was introduced by Commission members. However, such a bill was introduced by a non-Commission member, but the measure was never called.

During one of the Commission's public hearings, a witness pointed out that when it was necessary to increase the Township School Treasurer's bond because a school district had

issued bonds, the law required the Board of the district issuing the bonds to approve the increased bond of the Treasurer. The Commission recommended that since the Board of Trustees was the employer of the Treasurer and had to approve his original bond, that it should be the Trustees and not the School Board who should approve the increased bond. House Bill 34 was introduced in the 69th General Assembly in 1957 to implement this recommendation.[197]

Two other recommendations of the Commission were enacted into law at this session by passage of approval of House Bill 35. Election petitions of candidates for Trustees were to be filed twenty-one days prior to election day, rather than ten as previously provided; election for Township Trustees should be held on the second Saturday in April, the same as other elected school officers.[198]

Senate Bill 760 amended the act affecting Treasurers. In the event of a vacancy in that office caused by death, resignation, or removal from office, the School Board was to appoint a Treasurer for the unexpired term, rather than for a three-year term as the law had previously provided.[199] This amendment applied only to Class I counties; a similar provision was already in the law which applied to Class II counties. Another change required Treasurers to supply the School Board with a monthly reconciliation of cash balances. Further legislation repealed Section 14 which re-

quired the Treasurer to make an annual report.[200] This act also provided that any official convicted of falsely swearing to or affirming a report to be guilty of perjury.[201]

A general revision of the election code eliminated all Clerks of Elections in Townships and Districts.[202]

Legislative action in 1957 brought about a gradual loosening of the restrictions which the law had placed on School Boards regarding the sale and purchase of school property; Senate Bill 314 permitted the exchange of school sites without referendum when two-thirds of the Board felt that the exchange was equitable.[203] Senate Bill 775 permitted the sale without referendum, if two-thirds of the Board members considered the property unnecessary, unsuitable, or inconvenient because of reorganization.[204]

# 1959

Only two years after the passage of Senate Bills 324 and 775 (providing that sale of school property could be made under certain conditions), the General Assembly enacted House Bill 1519 which permitted such sales under any conditions if two-thirds of the School Board members were of the opinion that the property was unnecessary, unsuitable, or inconvenient for school use.[205]

Only two other measures which affected Trustees and Treasurers were enacted at the

1959 session. One, a Commission recommendation, provided that Township Land Commissioners, in addition to Treasurers, should loan school funds at interest.[206] The other was House Bill 712 which was proposed by a non-Commission member; it provided that for the election of School Trustees, the polls should be open from noon until 7:00 p.m.[207]

In its report to the General Assembly in 1961, the School Problems Commission recommended that only counties with a population of 1,000,000 (not 180,000) be Class II counties, thereby abolishing the offices of Township School Trustees and Treasurers in all counties but Cook. Several counties, in addition to Madison and St. Clair, had passed the 180,000 population in the 1960 census; had the law not been changed, those counties would have had to reinstate Township school officers. None of them wished to do that. This action gave added support to the efforts of the Commission for the previous ten years.

There was also a growing dissatisfaction with the old arrangement in St. Clair County. Two House members from St. Clair county joined Commission members as sponsors of House Bill 371 which was passed by the General Assembly on June 29 and approved by the Governor on August 15.[15] This legislation ended a controversy which had started many years before and which had been before the General Assembly in nearly every session since 1951.

A recodification of the school code was made in 1961, upon recommendation of the School Problems Commission, wherein laws affecting Trustees were moved from Article 4 to Article 5, and laws affecting Treasurers were moved from Article 5 to Article 8.

## 1963

In 1963, an attempt was made by three Cook County Democrats to abolish the Township School Offices in Cook County; the measure failed to clear the House Education Committee.[209]

The sponsors argued that by continuing those offices in Cook County, having abolished them downstate, was an act of discrimination against Cook County; the cost of the salary and the expense of operating those offices could be saved by such action.

Opponents argued that the conditions were distinctly different in Cook County than in the counties where abolition had occurred. Furthermore, they argued, this action had been taken in the 101 counties to eliminate hundreds of inactive and unneeded positions where the expense of running the offices was much greater than the income of the offices. Such was not the case in Cook County where the action this bill proposed would have greatly increased the number of Treasurers. To have more Treasurers doing the work previously performed by a few persons would cost much more, but the expense would be made up in the general expenses of the various districts. Finally, the current system of Township Treasurers permitted the investment of larger amounts of money, thereby generating more income, than would be realized from more but smaller amounts.

The controversy quickly became politically partisan, Democrats asking for the abolition and Republicans opposing. The General Assembly apparently thought that having an outside officer keep a separate check on the fiscal affairs of the school districts was good public administration.

A final resolution required that the annual financial statement of the school township be published in only one newspaper in the county; this resolution passed in the House but failed in the Senate.[210]

## 1965

In 1965, nine Democrats introduced House Bill 1944 which provided for the abolition of the offices of Trustees and Treasurers. It passed the House but failed in the Senate.[211] Also, introduced at that session was Senate Bill 1238 which would have abolished Trustees and had the Treasurers elected for a four-year term. It was not called in committee.[212] House Bill 1662 would have abolished the Trustees' office and had its function transferred to the board of town auditors.[213]

## 1973-1974

Several bills presented to the 78th General Assembly in 1973-74 dealt with Township Trustees and Treasurers.

House Bill 1416 proposed to reduce from two years to one year the length of time an unrecognized school might be maintained in a district without being automatically dissolved. It was enacted and became PA 78-508.[214] Senate Bill 787 prohibited a candidate for School Trustee from standing for both a full term and an unexpired term of office in the same election. One petition was to be withdrawn; this passed and became PA 78-657.[215]

Senate Bill 179 would have permitted Cook County school districts to appoint a Treasurer rather than utilize the services of the Township School Treasurer. This bill had Republican sponsorship and passed the Senate Education Committee, but was never called for a floor vote.

Most bills to abolish or reduce the functions of the offices of Trustees and Treasurers had Democratic sponsorship, perhaps because the political makeup of Suburban Cook County was Republican and therefore most Treasurers were Republican. However, an increasing number of bills had either bi-partisan or Republican sponsorships indicative of another force working to alter the system. This other force was school administrators who wanted the Treasurers appointed by the School Boards and wanted the functions of the Trustees assumed by the County Boards of School Trustees.[216]

## 1977

In August of 1977, the legislature further clarified the qualifications for Treasurer and the administration of his duties. In addition to fulfilling the requirements set by previous law, ". . . each Treasurer appointed . . . after the effective date of [this Act], . . . [was to] have a financial background or related experience or twelve semester hours of credit at college-level accounting."[217] The new legislation also clearly stated the Treasurer's responsibilities for the administration of duties. As of August 1977, the Treasurer was to "be responsible for receipts, disbursements and investments arising out of the operation of the school district under his supervision."[218]

No other legislation affecting Trustees or Treasurers was approved by this General Assembly.

# Conclusion: A Plan for Today and the Future

Recent years have witnessed attempted legislation which, if passed, would have directly affected the offices of Trustee and Treasurer. It would seem appropriate to conclude this study by examining briefly some of this legislation in order to focus public attention on public issues. In addition, the nature of these issues reflects the attitude of the Trustees and Treasurers toward their own offices and responsibilities as well as toward the people.

Current law calls for Trustees and Treasurers to meet semi-annually. An effort was made to change these mandatory meetings to a quarterly basis. The more-frequent meetings, theoretically, would have led to an increased communication and understanding between the Treasurers and the Trustees. Furthermore, the increased contact should have led to an increase in office involvement, as well as the upgrading of services, as might be expected from an increase in contact and communication. It was the consensus of opinion that such legislative action would have improved the organization. The bill was passed out of committee, but died on the House floor; its death is most likley attributable to its appearance before the House at the end of a frantic session of the General Assembly. In all likelihood, the bill will reappear at a future session.

A second bill which failed to clear the committee dealt with the location of the Treasurer's office. As fixed by law, the Treasurer must reside in but does not have to maintain an office in the township which he serves. For example, it would be possible for a Treasurer to serve suburban Cook County, yet, if he desired, he could maintain his office in downtown Chicago instead of in his township. The proposed legislation would have required the Treasurer to maintain an office in his township. This bill is also most likely to be reintroduced in a future session.

Other future legislation that the Trustees and Treasurers support reflects their honest attempts to further increase the professionalism and integrity of their offices. For example, many officers are in favor of passing legislation that would establish a clear-cut, lockstep procedure for dealing with a non-functioning Treasurer. Current laws are somewhat vague and slightly ineffective. What seems to be favored is a law which would require the County Superintendent to take action against a non-functioning Treasurer. This new procedure would necessitate the Superintendent's bringing said Treasurer's office into conformity with the law.

Several changes in the operation of the offices of Treasurer and Trustee also reflect changes in the philosophy and administration of these offices. In its early days, the office of Treasurer, for example, operated under an unwritten law of strict economy, especially in regard to office equipment expenses. Recent times find no fewer than seven Treasurers sharing computer facilities, programs, and programmers. The amount of data and information readily available greatly increases the service and flexibility that the Treasurers can offer their school systems. At the same time, the shared facilities and personnel keep operating costs at a minimum, an important factor considering the current economic environment and its relation to educational programs and expenses. Thus, these Trustees have combined their original desire for economy with the benefits of advancing technology.

This concern for economy is also evident in the Treasurers' attempts to minimize the amount of paper work within the schools and school systems themselves. For example, the Treasurer is the legal financial officer for the schools and school districts and, as such, is required by law to keep financial records. This includes all reporting of financial matters by the schools to the state or federal governments. The accurate, required record keeping by the Treasurer should free the schools and school systems of this record keeping and thereby prevent the duplication of work, and more importantly, realize a substantial economic savings.

As this report has shown, from their inception, the offices of Trustee and Treasurer have been respected and viable forces in the history of the Illinois educational system. The modern-day office holders share with their predecessors the desire to provide this state with quality schools and school districts.

# END NOTES

1. *Laws of Illinois 1819* (Springfield: State of Illinois, 1820), p. 107.

2. Ibid., p. 108.

3. Illinois Education Association, *Building the State Common School Fund in Illinois* (Springfield: IEA, 1943).

4. *Laws of Illinois, First Session of First General Assembly* (Springfield: State of Illinois, n.d.), p. 107.

5. *United States Statutes at Large* (Washington, D.C.: U.S. Printing Office, n.d.), 3:29C.

6. *Laws of Illinois, First Session of First General Assembly,* p. 107.

7. Ibid., p. 85.

8. Victor H. Sheppherd, *A Brief History of the Office of Public Instruction*

9. *Laws Passed by the Second General Assembly of Illinois* (Springfield: State of Illinois, n.d.), p. 41.

10. *Laws of Illinois, First Session of Second General Assembly Commenced at Vandalia December 4, 1820* (Springfield: State of Illinois, n.d.), p. 154.

11. Illinois Education Association, *Building the State Common School Fund in Illinois.*

12. Sheppherd, *Brief History,* p. 11.

13. Paul E. Belting, *Development of the Free Public High School in Illinois* (1900), p. 97.

14. Ibid., p. 97.

15. *Laws of Illinois 1825* (Springfield: State of Illinois, 1826), p. 121.

16. Ibid., p. 121.

17. Ibid., p. 121.

18. Ibid., p. 122.

19. Ibid., p. 123.

20. Ibid., pp. 123-124.

21. Ibid., p. 124.

22. *Laws of Illinois 1823-1825* (Springfield: State of Illinois, 1826), p. 125.

23. Ibid., p. 126.

24. Ibid., p. 126.

25. Belting, p. 101.

26. Ibid., p. 102.

27. *Laws of Illinois 1826-1827* (Springfield: State of Illinois, 1828), p. 79.

28. *Revised Laws of 1827* (Springfield: State of Illinois, 1827) p. 365.

29. Ibid., p. 365.

30. Ibid., p. 365.

31. Ibid., p. 366.

32. Ibid., p. 368.

33. Ibid., p. 369.

34. *Revised Laws of 1829* (Springfield: State of Illinois, 1829), p. 149.

35. Ibid., p. 149.

36. Ibid., p. 150.

37. Ibid., p. 150.

38. Ibid., p. 154.

39. Ibid., p. 154.

40. Ibid., p. 118.

41. Belting, p. 107

42. *Laws of Illinois 1831* (Springfield: State of Illinois, 1832), p. 173.

43. Ibid., p. 175.

44. Ibid., p. 176.

45. Ibid., p. 173.

46. Ibid., p. 173.

47. *Laws of Illinois 1833* (Springfield, State of Illinois, 1834), p. 562.

48. Ibid., p. 562.

49. *Laws of Illinois 1835* (Springfield: State of Illinois, 1836), p. 249.

50. In 1969 it was reduced to $28,500. and omitted entirely in PA 76-2559 in 1970.

51. *Laws in Illinois 1837* (Springfield: State of Illinois, 1838), pp. 315-316.

52. Ibid., pp. 318-319.

53. Ibid., p. 20.

54. Ibid., pp. 316-317.

55. Ibid., p. 317.

56. Ibid., p. 315.

57. Ibid., p. 318.

58. Ibid., p. 319.

59. *Laws in Illinois 1841* (Springfield: State of Illinois, 1842), pp. 259-260.

60. Ibid., p. 260.

61. Ibid., pp. 261-263 and pp. 267-269.

62. Ibid., p. 269.

63. Ibid., pp. 269-270.

64. Ibid., p. 269.

65. Ibid., pp. 273-275.

66. Ibid., p. 276.

67. Ibid., pp. 276-279.

68. Ibid., p. 279.

69. Ibid., p. 282.

70. *Smith-Hurd Annotated Statutes* (St. Paul: West Pub. Co., 1961), p. 139.

71. Ibid., p. 142.

72. Ibid., p. 139.

73. *Laws of Illinois 1841,* p. 283.

74. Ibid., p. 285.

75. *Laws of Illinois 1843,* (Springfield: State of Illinois, 1844), p. 271.

76. Sheppherd, *Brief History,* p. 17.

77. Ibid., p. 18.

78. *Laws of Illinois 1845* (Springfield: State of Illinois, 1846), p. 54.

79. Ibid., p. 57.

80. Ibid., p. 59.

81. *Report of School Problems Commission #1* (Springfield: State of Illinois, 1951), p. 83, and *Laws of Illinois 1845,* p. 64.

82. *Laws of Illinois 1845,* p. 60.

83. Ibid., p. 61.

84. Ibid., p. 61 and p. 73.

85. Ibid., p. 61.

86. Ibid., pp. 61-62

87. Ibid., p. 63.

88. Ibid., p. 64.

89. Ibid., p. 70.

90. Ibid., p. 69.

91. Ibid., p. 71.

92. Ibid., p. 71.

93. Ibid., p. 73.

94. *Smith-Hurd,* p. 139.

95. *Laws of Illinois 1847* (Springfield: State of Illinois, 1848), p. 149.

96. Ibid., p. 127.

97. Ibid., p. 130 and p. 126.

98. Ibid., pp. 127-128

99. Ibid., p. 128.

100. Ibid., p. 131 and p. 141.

101. Ibid., p. 139.

102. *Laws of Illinois 1845* p. 72.

103. *Laws of Illinois 1847* p. 146.

104. *Laws of Illinois 1849* (Springfield: State of Illinois, 1850), p. 162.

105. Ibid., p. 177.

106. Ibid., p. 179.

107. *Laws of Illinois 1855* (Springfield: State of Illinois, 1856), p. 77.

108. Ibid., p. 79.

109. Ibid., p. 80.

110. Ibid., p. 81.

111. Sheppard, *History of the Office of State Superintendent,* p. 38.

112. Ibid., p. 40.

113. Shepperd, *Brief History,* pp. 28-29.

114. *Laws of Illinois 1855* p. 60.

115. Ibid., p. 60.

116. Ibid., p. 70.

117. *Laws of Illinois 1857* (Springfield: State of Illinois, 1858), p. 268.

118. *Laws of Illinois 1861* (Springfield: State of Illinois, 1862), p. 188.

119. Ibid., p. 188.

120. *Laws of Illinois 1857* p. 269.

121. Ibid., pp. 271-272.

122. *Smith-Hurd,* p. 122.

123. *Laws of Illinois 1859* (Springfield: State of Illinois, 1860), p. 160.

124. Ibid., p. 161.

125. *Laws of Illinois 1865* (Springfield: State of Illinois, 1866), p. 115.

126. Ibid., p. 121.

127. *Laws of Illinois 1869* (Springfield: State of Illinois, 1870), p. 393.

128. Illinois Education Association, *The School Township Problem in Illinois* (Springfield: IEA, 1950),
p. 7.

129. *Laws of Illinois 1871-72* (Springfield: State of Illinois, 1873), p. 706.

130. *Laws of Illinois 1872* (Springfield: State of Illinois, 1873), p. 713.

131. *Laws of Illinois 1879* (Springfield: State of Illinois, 1880), p. 294.

132. *Laws of Illinois 1847* (Springfield: State of Illinois, 1890), p. 277.

133. *Laws of Illinois 1871-72,* p. 710.

134. *Laws of Illinois 1877* (Springfield: State of Illinois, 1878), p. 201.

135. *Laws of Illinois 1871-72* p. 714.

136. Ibid., p. 707.

137. Ibid., p. 700.

138. Ibid., p. 393.

139. Ibid., p. 728.

140. *Laws of Illinois 1877* p. 201.

141. *Revised Statutes of Illinois 1877* (Springfield: State of Illinois, 1878), p. 1211.

142. *Statutes of Illinois 1872* (Springfield: State of Illinois, 1873), p. 408.

143. *Laws of Illinois 1879* p. 306.

144. *Laws of Illinois 1883* (Springfield: State of Illinois, 1884), pp. 164-165.

145. *Laws of Illinois 1929* (Springfield: State of Illinois, 1930), p. 293.

146. *Laws of Illinois 1889* p. 270.

147. Ibid., p. 268.

148. *Laws of Illinois 1891* (Springfield: State of Illinois, 1892), p. 135.

149. Ibid., p. 196.

150. *Smith-Hurd Annotated Statutes of the School Code of 1861,* p. 40.

151. *Laws of Illinois 1899* (Springfield: State of Illinois, 1890), p. 375.

152. *Laws of Illinois 1905* (Springfield: State of Illinois, 1906), p. 378.

153. *Smith-Hurd Annotated Statutes,* p. 149 note.

154. *Laws of Illinois 1909* (Springfield: State of Illinois, 1910), p. 360.

155. Ibid., p. 363.

156. *Smith-Hurd Revised Statutes* (St. Paul, Minn.: West Pub. Co., 1929), p. 2602.

157. Ibid., p. 2601.

158. Ibid., p. 2602.

159. *Laws of Illinois 1935* (Springfield: State of Illinois, 1936), p. 1392.

160. *Illinois Legislative Synopsis and Digest* (Springfield: State of Illinois, 1935), p. 296.

161. *Illinois Legislative Synopsis and Digest* (Springfield: State of Illinois, 1937), p. 137.

162. *Laws of Illinois 1939* (Springfield: State of Illinois, 1940), p. 1118.

163. *Laws of Illinois 1941* (Springfield: State of Illinois, 1942), p. 1200.

164. Ibid., p. 1200.

165. *Laws of Illinois 1943* (Springfield: State of Illinois, 1944), p. 1296.

166. Ibid., p. 1298.

167. *Laws of Illinois 1945* (Springfield: State of Illinois, 1946), p. 1346.

168. *Laws of Illinois 1953* (Springfield: State of Illinois, 1954), p. 1366.

169. *Laws of Illinois 1945* (Springfield: State of Illinois, 1946), pp. 1343-1345.

170. *Laws of Illinois 1949* (Springfield: State of Illinois, 1950), p. 1402.

171. *Illinois Legislative Synopsis and Digest* (Springfield: State of Illinois, 1949), p. 222.

172. *Report of School Problems Commission #1, pp. 41-42.*

173. *Ibid., p. 83.*

174. *Ibid., pp. 83-84*

175. *Ibid., p. 84.*

176. *Ibid., p. 86.*

177. *Ibid., p. 83.*

178. *Ibid., p. 84.*

179. *Ibid., p. 87.*

180. *Ibid., p. 87.*

181. *Ibid., p. 87-88.*

182. *Ibid., p. 88.*

183. *Ibid., pp. 16-19.*

184. *Legislative Final Legislative Synopsis and Digest* (Springfield: State of Illinois, 1951).

185. *Laws of Illinois 1951* (Springfield: State of Illinois, 1952), pp. 1807, 1982-1993.

186. Ibid., p. 1416.

187. *Report of School Problems Commission #2* (Springfield: State of Illinois, n.d.), p. 19.

188. Ibid., p. 19.

189. Ibid., p. 19.

190. Ibid., p. 19.

191. Ibid., p. 20.

192. *Laws of Illinois 1953* pp. 1418-1421.

193. Ibid., p. 1419.

194. *Laws of Illinois 1953* pp. 1401-1417 and 1422.

195. *Illinois Legislative Synopsis and Digest* (Springfield: State of Illinois, 1953).

196. *Laws of Illinois 1955* (Springfield: State of Illinois, 1956), p. 1325.

197. *Report of School Problems Commission #4* (Springfield: State of Illinois, n.d.), p. 9, and *Laws of Illinois 1957* (Springfield: State of Illinois), p. 211.

198. Ibid., p. 9 and Ibid., pp. 212-213.

199. *Laws of Illinois 1957* p. 2868.

200. Ibid., p. 2868.

201. Ibid., p. 2865.

202. Ibid., p. 1450.

203. Ibid., p. 287.

204. Ibid., p. 1217.

205. *Laws of Illinois 1959* (Springfield: State of Illinois, 1960), p. 2057.

206. Ibid., p. 2049.

207. Ibid., p. 1196.

208. *Laws of Illinois 1961* (Springfield: State of Illinois, 1962), p. 3370.

209. *Illinois Legislative Synopsis and Digest* (Springfield: State of Illinois, 1963), p. 802.

210. Ibid., p. 750.

211. *Illinois Legislative Synopsis and Digest* (Springfield: State of Illinois, 1965), p. 945.

212. Ibid., p. 346.

213. Ibid., p. 854.

214. *Laws of Illinois 1973-74* (Springfield: State of Illinois, 1975), p. 1438.

215. Ibid., pp. 1945-1949.

216. *Illinois Legislative Synopsis and Digest* (Springfield: State of Illinois, 1973-1974), p. 103.

217. *Laws of Illinois 1977* (Springfield: State of Illinois, 1978), p. 1105.

218. Ibid., p. 1105.

# BIBLIOGRAPHY

Belting, Paul E. *Development of the Free Public High School in Illinois.*

Illinois Education Association. *Building the State Common School Fund in Illinois.* Springfield: IEA, 1943.

Illinois Education Association. *The School Township Problem in Illinois.* Springfield: IEA, 1950.

*Illinois Legislative Synopsis and Digest.* Springfield: State of Illinois, 1935.

*Illinois Legislative Synopsis and Digest.* Springfield: State of Illinois, 1937.

*Illinois Legislative Synopsis and Digest.* Springfield: State of Illinois, 1949.

*Illinois Legislative Synopsis and Digest.* Springfield: State of Illinois, 1953.

*Illinois Legislative Synopsis and Digest.* Springfield: State of Illinois, 1963.

*Illinois Legislative Synopsis and Digest.* Springfield: State of Illinois, 1965.

*Illinois Legislative Synopsis and Digest.* Springfield: State of Illinois, 1973-1974.

*Laws of Illinois 1819.* Springfield: State of Illinois, 1820.

*Laws of Illinois 1823-1825.* Springfield: State of Illinois, 1826.

*Laws of Illinois 1825.* Springfield: State of Illinois, 1826.

*Laws of Illinois 1826-1827.* Springfield: State of Illinois, 1828.

*Laws of Illinois 1831.* Springfield: State of Illinois, 1832.

*Laws of Illinois 1833.* Springfield: State of Illinois, 1834.

*Laws of Illinois 1835.* Springfield: State of Illinois, 1836.

*Laws of Illinois 1837.* Springfield: State of Illinois, 1838.

*Laws of Illinois 1841.* Springfield: State of Illinois, 1842.

*Laws of Illinois 1843.* Springfield: State of Illinois, 1844.

*Laws of Illinois 1845.* Springfield: State of Illinois, 1846.

*Laws of Illinois 1847.* Springfield: State of Illinois, 1848.

*Laws of Illinois 1849.* Springfield: State of Illinois, 1850.

*Laws of Illinois 1855.* Springfield: State of Illinois, 1856.

*Laws of Illinois 1857.* Springfield: State of Illinois, 1858.

*Laws of Illinois 1859.* Springfield: State of Illinois, 1860.

*Laws of Illinois 1861.* Springfield: State of Illinois, 1862.

*Laws of Illinois 1865.* Springfield: State of Illinois, 1866.

*Laws of Illinois 1869.* Springfield: State of Illinois, 1870.

*Laws of Illinois 1871-1872.* Springfield: State of Illinois, 1873.

*Laws of Illinois 1872.* Springfield: State of Illinois, 1873.

*Laws of Illinois 1877.* Springfield: State of Illinois, 1878.

*Laws of Illinois 1879.* Springfield: State of Illinois, 1880.

*Laws of Illinois 1883.* Springfield: State of Illinois, 1884

*Laws of Illinois 1889.* Springfield: State of Illinois, 1890.

*Laws of Illinois 1891.* Springfield: State of Illinois, 1892.

*Laws of Illinois 1899.* Springfield: State of Illinois, 1900.

*Laws of Illinois 1905.* Springfield: State of Illinois, 1906.

*Laws of Illinois 1909.* Springfield: State of Illinois, 1910.

*Laws of Illinois 1929.* Springfield: State of Illinois, 1930.

*Laws of Illinois 1935.* Springfield: State of Illinois, 1936.

*Laws of Illinois 1939.* Springfield: State of Illinois, 1940.

*Laws of Illinois 1941.* Springfield: State of Illinois, 1942.

*Laws of Illinois 1943.* Springfield: State of Illinois, 1944.

*Laws of Illinois 1945.* Springfield: State of Illinois, 1946.

*Laws of Illinois 1949.* Springfield: State of Illinois, 1950.

*Laws of Illinois 1951.* Springfield: State of Illinois, 1952.

*Laws of Illinois 1953.* Springfield: State of Illinois, 1954.

*Laws of Illinois 1955.* Springfield: State of Illinois, 1956.

*Laws of Illinois 1957.* Springfield: State of Illinois, 1958.

*Laws of Illinois 1959.* Springfield: State of Illinois, 1960.

*Laws of Illinois 1961.* Springfield: State of Illinois, 1962.

*Laws of Illinois 1973-1974.* Springfield: State of Illinois, 1975.

*Laws of Illinois 1977.* Springfield: State of Illinois, 1978.

*Laws of Illinois, First Session of First General Assembly.* Springfield: State of Illinois, n.d.

*Laws of Illinois, First Session of Second General Assembly Commenced at Vandalia December 4, 1820.* Springfield: State of Illinois, n.d.

*Laws Passed by the Second General Assembly of Illinois.* Springfield: State of Illinois, n.d.

*Legislative Final Legislative Synopsis and Digest.* Springfield: State of Illinois, 1951.

*Report of School Problems Commission #1.* Springfield: State of Illinois, 1951.

*Report of School Problems Commission #2.* Springfield: State of Illinois, n.d.

*Report of the School Problems Commission #4.* Springfield: State of Illinois, n.d.

*Revised Laws of 1827.* Springfield: State of Illinois, 1827.

*Revised Laws of 1829.* Springfield: State of Illinois, 1829.

Sheppard. *History of the Office of State Superintendent.*

Sheppherd, Victor H. A Brief History of the Office of Public Instruction.

Smith-Hurd Annotated Statutes. St. Paul, Minn: West Publishing Company, 1961.

*Smith-Hurd Annotated Statutes of the School Code of 1861.*

*Smith-Hurd Revised Statutes.* St. Paul, Minn.: 1929

*United States Statutes at Large.* 3:29C.